MODELS OF

FAITH

Biblical Spirituality for Our Time

Carlos G. Valles, S.J.

A Campion Book

Loyola University Press
Chicago, Illinois

Loyola University Press
3441 North Ashland Avenue
Chicago, Illinois 60657

Library of Congress Cataloging - in - Publication Data

Valesa, Father, 1925 -
    Models of faith: biblical spirituality for our day / by Carlos G.
  Valles.
        p. cm.
    Reprint. Originally published: Anand, Gujurat, India: Gujurat
  Sahitya Prakash.
    ISBN 0-8294-0707-3
    1. Faith--Biblical teaching. 2. Christian life--Catholic authors.
  I. Title
  BS680.F27V34 1990
  234'.2--dc20   90-36518
                                                           CIP

CONTENTS

GET THEE OUT

Faith begins with Abraham. "Get thee out." The divine command that breaks into the biblical narrative after creation and the flood and the dispersion brought about by the pride of Babel, and opens up a new path for mankind in the land of Harran. "Leave your own country, your kinsmen, and your father's house, and go to a country which I will show you." (Gn 12:1). This is the essential movement of faith: the break with the familiar past, and the bold march into an unknown future. Leave your people, your land, your home, all that makes for security and safety and comfort in the face of the desert, leave life as you know it, leave behind you your way of thinking, your traditions, your ways of looking at things and evaluating persons and pursuing goals; leave behind you your own past, get started, move on, go ahead. The anchoring power of man's memories, tastes, beliefs, habits, relations and possessions is overwhelming, but the word of faith cuts through it all and sets the mind free for a new adventure under the divine summons. And Abraham, who was seventy-five years old by then, took with him his wife Sarai and his nephew Lot with family and dependants, and started off on his journey.

1

Where to? "To a country which I will show you." That is the test of faith, its peculiar demand, its very essence. Faith does not reveal the end of the journey. It keeps it dark and hidden and remote. It does not tell from the beginning all that will happen at the end. It works on trust, it keeps man waiting, it delays the revelation. Get going and I shall let you know. For the moment all you know is that you are to get out of where you are and to start in this direction. You will receive further instructions as you go along. Do not ask now, do not beg for explanations, do not expect certainties. Action first, justifications later. Start your journey, and never mind what the last stop will be. Trust the voice that calls you, and wait for it to call you again when you are on your way. One stage at a time. One step at a time. Difficult to take for him who wants to know where his last step will take him before he takes the first.

Abraham's leave-taking from his neighbours must have been a rather amusing one, unless he left at dead of night. Where was he going? they must have asked as he gathered his possessions, filled the sacks and loaded the asses. He knew well, of course, ways of hiding the truth, and later in Egypt he would say that his wife was his sister in order to protect himself; but if he wanted to give a straight answer, it would be greeted by smiling lips and frowning brows all round. Starting tomorrow, and not knowing where? That is a strange way for a sensible man to go. And yet that was all he knew. Except that in his very being he sensed the certainty, beyond all human assurances, that steadied his heart and lit in darkness his mind. In that light he could go, even if those around him saw in his going only the questionable adventure of an unsteady spirit.

Man in a calculating animal. He wants guarantees, certainties, clear conditions and definite gains. If he is to start

2

on a journey, and more so on a long journey through a hostile desert, he wants at least a map, a route, a detailed sketch, a reliable guide. Where do I start, where does the first halt come, how long can I stay, where do I go from there, how many stages to my journey, where do I finally reach and how long will I take to get there...? Without that information no serious person will undertake an important journey. But Abraham will be given none of that. And he will start all the same. Faith does not ask questions. It starts, it moves, it obeys. The shadow, the veil, the night. It asks for no blue-print, and requires no estimates. Man's nature is to ask for a contract and to demand insurance. It is satisfied only with concrete conditions and definite clauses. It wants to know, to grasp, to be informed in full, to be given details so that it can consider and weigh and decide. Yet that advance information is denied him in the transactions of faith. He has to make a choice without mastering the case; he has to start on his way without knowing the final destination. "By faith Abraham obeyed the call to go out to a land destined for himself and his heirs, and left home without knowing where he was to go." (Heb 11:8). That commitment to action beyond the grasp of the intellect is the mark of the believer, and the bold march into the unknown was what made Abraham the father of all believers.

God seems to like particularly this way of dealing with men, asking his faithful servants to start on an errand with only initial directives, reserving fuller information for a later date which he leaves unspecified. Samuel was entrusted with the responsibility of anointing a new king in Israel, and these were the instructions he received: "Fill your horn with oil and take it with you; I am sending you to Jesse of Bethlehem...; you shall anoint for me there the man whom I shall show you." (1 Sm 16). The prophet started at once on

3

his blind errand. He knew well the ways of God, and tried his skills while he watched for the sign. Seven times he missed with seven sons of Jesse, thinking each one in turn to be the chosen one. It was only when young David was summoned from the fields that Samuel heard the words: "Rise and anoint him: this is the man." And his mission was completed.

John the Baptist had a similar experience. He was asked to announce the arrival of the Messiah, though "I myself did not know who he was." (Jn 1:31). He did proclaim in faith the coming of one whose sandals he was not worthy to unfasten, till he himself was shown, with the sign of the dove and the voice from heaven, the person of the Chosen One, and was able to point with outstretched arm and announce with final authority: "This is the Lamb of God, the one who takes away the sin of the world."

And again Paul, when struck by grace on the road to Damascus, was also asked to start a new life, though he was not given there and then the details of it. The only directive was, "Get up and go into the city, and you will be told what you have to do." (Ac 9:6). That is the attitude of faith: get up, go, and you will be told. You will be shown the place, you will be taken to the person, you will be guided. Do not ask questions, but start moving right now, or you will get nowhere. The test of faith, its very essence and definition, is to start a new life on God's word, to journey into the unknown and to risk the future without asking for assurances, guarantees, detailed loans or advance information. "Go ahead, and I will show you." Is not our vocation, our call, our consecration to God for life a similar experience in faith? Do we know when we start where we are going to reach? Do we guess the future that awaits us, and do we ask to know? No. We also receive God's

4

command in the depth of our hearts, we take leave of whatever world was ours, and we depart. On his word we go.

God is the Master of the human mind, the Lord of life and history, and the act of faith recognizes him precisely as supreme Lord and absolute Master. Man surrenders before him his very right to know where he is going, his right to understand what he can expect, to be given conditions and to sign pacts. Man surrenders his understanding, his future, his life, and in doing so he recognizes God, in deed and in action, as the Lord of the universe, and sees in God's word a stronger support than all his own planning and earning and foreseeing could ever win for him. The act of faith is the supreme compliment man in his finitude can pay almighty God in his majesty. To trust his word, to believe his promise, to pack his belongings (the luggage of the mind, much heavier than the one carried by Abraham's asses), and to commit his whole life to God by moving, literally heart and soul, body and mind, present and future, in the direction to which God's finger points. In faith there is assent, trust and commitment. In faith there is the whole of man acting totally at the single command of his God and Master. That is why faith is the very basis of all religion.

If the merit of faith is the stepping out into the unknown, its reward is the very promise of God who engages his own fidelity and truthfulness in assuring the faithful servant bliss and joy beyond what he can imagine or expect: "I will make you into a great nation, I will bless you and make your name great. All the families on earth will pray to be blessed as you are blessed." (Gn 12:2). If Abraham does not know where he is going, he does know that he will be blessed beyond reckoning, and his descendants with him. What shape God's blessing will take

5

he does not exactly know, but he trusts his bounty and generosity, and in that promise he finds strength and purpose to go ahead against all odds.

God's promise is the guiding light of man's life. As promise, it is the attitude that befits God: free, generous and all-embracing. The king's good-pleasure, his mercy and his grace. God pledges his word, and man rejoices in the expectation of a reward far beyond his merits and high above his hopes. God's promise is firmer and stronger than any contract, than any claim, than any demand man could make as payment for his virtue and his obedience. "You will be blessed" is the happiest declaration man can hear, coming from God at the beginning of his eventful journey. Everything becomes possible and everything turns out easy when God's blessing waits at the end. Abraham knew.

Every journey into the unknown is an act of faith, whether the traveller realizes it or not. And man's greatest journey, image and beginning of all his other journeys through life and into eternity, is his own birth. That is the great departure, the great adventure, the great migration. Man's birth from his mother's womb is also an answer to God's command through the laws of nature and of life: "Get thee out." Come out of the safety of the womb into a new and strange land which I will show you. Nothing stranger in creation than the land that is this world and the adventure that is human life. But it also comes with the promise and the blessing. The supreme blessing for him who believes and sets out and journeys forth and embraces life with all its joys and sorrows and light and shadows and risks and fulfilment in God's own time and God's own way. True, we are not consulted at the time of birth, and it is not our free choice to be born, but once we become conscious and free we can ratify and accept our birth with willingness and readiness of heart, making our own God's decision to send us into this world. In fact that is what we do every time we celebrate our birthday and accept gifts and congratulations for the fact of being alive. Every birthday party is a joyful answer to God's initial call, a colourful act of obedience to the first command that brought us into life. We religious have the custom of renewing our vows every year, deepening each time our commitment as the experience of life brings understanding to the meaning of our poverty, chastity and obedience, making up as we advance in years and in wisdom for the incompleteness of our first generosity in the impulse of youth. In a similar way every birthday celebration is a renewal of vows, a conscious acceptance in faith and joy of the responsibility of having been born, a Yes to life and therefore to God who gave it in the first instance, a new departure, a confirmation for the onward journey. As we accept our baptism, though most of us were not conscious of it when the waters were poured on our heads, so we accept our birth year by year and day by day by living joyfully the life we have once been given and granted till now. To continue the journey with love is the best way to express our gratitude for its ever having begun.

The call of faith is not once and for all. It comes again and again in man's life, demanding more each time, making concrete the first general call to life in daily events and in formal choices, leading him ever higher and ever closer to the final goal of the journey. Abraham himself saw the call repeated in his life. His faith was tested again and again, and we know some of the tests he went through, reminders and renewals of the first departure into the desert. He was asked to believe that he could have a son from his wife in spite of the "deadness of Sarah's womb" who laughed when she heard the prophecy; and he was asked to believe that his descendants would be blessed even as he was required to sacrifice the life of the very son from whom those descendants had to come. God calls again and again, and faith is kept alive by the trials of life and the vicissitudes of human existence.

The calls of faith. Big and small. The decisive occasions that mark a man's life, and the passing events that build up the day in anonymous succession of delicate graces. Every step is an act of faith, every morning is a surprise and every sunrise a challenge. To sit in a plane is an act of faith, to open a door is an act of faith, to shake a hand is an act of faith, to smile into an unknown face is an act of faith. To face life is faith, is the daily journey into the unknown, and if we learn to actualize moment by moment the one great vocation of our original call into existence, to see in each small step the instant summary of the lifelong journey, to vivify each experience with the memory of God's command and the renewal of his promise, we can transform our life into a life of faith as true descendants of Abraham. He is our father in the faith.

MEET THE BOSS

Rabindranath Tagore had an experience, when he was young, which helped him later in life to realize himself and to describe to others what faith is and the role it plays in man's life. When he was a boy, he says, his eyes were weak, he saw things rather blurred and indistinct as his eyesight was defective. But he did not know that his vision was faulty, he did not know that his situation was abnormal, he thought that was the way things were seen, the way everybody saw them with fuzzy outlines and unclear background, and so he never thought of saying anything about it, of complaining to his parents or seeking a remedy. He certainly saw enough to recognize people when they came close, to find his way around the house and around town, to play with his friends and kick the ball when it came within reach; and with that imperfect sight he carried on for years without suspecting that it was deficient. He was shortsighted from birth, but he did not know it.

One day, he later reminisced, he was playing with other boys, one of whom wore spectacles. He then, in jest, took the other boy's spectacles and tried them on. And then a miracle happened. For the first time in his life he saw clearly, neatly, distinctly. he could see far with perfect clarity and near with absolute precision. He saw as he was always meant to see, as other men always saw, and as things were in themselves, with colour and line and shades and perspective, with depth and realism, with movement and sharpness, with sudden charm and unsuspected beauty. Everything fell simultaneously into place before his bewildered eyes and his astonished mind. His first real view of a colourful world, of smiling faces and playful children, of trees and birds, of deep blue sky and moving clouds. And as he saw all that in an outburst of wonder, he experienced two clear opposite feelings, so marked and definite that he could clearly remember them when many years later he relived that experience in a prayer talk in Santiniketan to draw from it an inspired lesson on the meaning of faith.

The first feeling, he said, was one of irrepressible joy and exultation at seeing for the first time such a beautiful world with such perfection of exact lines and multiple colours, a joy that was to stay with him for life and be reflected in his poems and his stories and his talks and his essays, in his understanding of life and in his relationship with God in tender devotion and enlightened surrender as loving Lord and provident Father. And then the second feeling, as sharp and strong as the first, though in a way opposite to it and deeply disturbing. A feeling of sadness and anger, almost of indignation against himself and forceful protest against whatever it was in him and in the world that had kept him ignorant of such a beauty till then. What a fool I was that I have been missing such a wonderful view all my life till this moment! The world was beautiful, and I did not know it! All things had shapes and colours and movement and life, and I was in the midst of it all and missing all the

10

fun, all the art and all the charm around me. How can I have been so dull for so long, and how can I make up now for such a loss!

And then the lesson. The application of this personal parable. The world is... the world. My eyes are... my eyes: feeble and weak and imperfect though I do not know it yet. And the spectacles are... faith. In fact there is a Sanskrit word to describe the role of the religious outlook in the life of man *divyachakshu:* "the divine eye". A new vision, a divine angle, a heavenly perspective of things and persons and events. Without it I can live somehow and feel my way around and guess faces and tread paths, but all in a shadow, a cloud, a blur. It is a drab world and a dull existence. And I, in my ignorance, believe that that is the normal way to see, the way all see and the way things are in themselves, that that is all life has to offer and there is no more to it. And so I live a resigned, subdued, limited existence with dimmed joys and faded perspectives. Then I call it life, and I complain of its being monotonous and grey and boring beyond endurance. Nothing makes sense, nothing attracts, appeals, relieves the sheer drudgery of living. It is only when faith comes into my life that all that is changed, that things fall into place and acquire colour and shape, that everything makes sense and the world is beautiful and creation is friendly and life is worth living and I can enjoy playing its games and walking its paths and scanning its horizons with a new light and a new joy. The divine eye. Looking at things as God looks at them. And I will be the loser if I miss the wondrous spectacle that can be mine if only I am ready to accept the gift, to try on my playmate's spectacles for once.

Tagore's experience reminded me of the person who, in the early days of colour TV, complained that there must be some faulty connexion as he was not getting the colour

11

programmes on his set. As a matter of fact his set was only black-and-white, and he did not know he had to buy a different and more expensive set if he wanted to see colour on the screen. Again figure and image of the same situation: life in itself is a full-colour programme, but if my TV set is only black-and-white (and in fact more black than white!) I shall miss the colour, and shall see only black shadows on my screen. The fault is not with the programme or with the station or with the connection, but with my set. I shall have to make a new investment if I want to see colour at home.

To see things as God sees them. That is faith. And that is not easy. At least it is not common, not usual, not the ordinary way we look at things and interpret events. In faith, every event that takes place around me is God's will for me, and as such is salvific, adorable, messenger of God's love for me and instrument of my growth and progress in grace. But I often miss the message, ignore its origin and curse the event. Why should I suffer, why should this happen to me, what is the meaning of all this misery, why is life so cruel and death so threatening and people so senseless and creation so empty? The world is in a mess and mankind is at a loss, and I am caught in the middle of this absurd performance, unable to make sense of anything and to justify things for which I, in my shortsightedness, see no justification. I complain, I rebel, I protest. I feel indignant at world news, and impatient at personal trials; I chafe at reality and disown history, I find fault with everything, and my mind does not rest at ease in creation.

We have it on record that when God looked at the world he had created, he was pleased with his work and repeatedly declared that it was good, indeed very good. We now look at the same world and unhesitatingly proclaim it to be a hopeless mess. True, things have happened on earth since creation, but, again in God's view, redemption is even more glorious than creation, and redeemed man a greater wonder than merely created man. Whatever has happened to mankind is part of God's beneficent plan, though that is not our first impression when we read the morning paper or watch the evening news on TV. We do not accept the world as it is (acceptance meaning also work for change and progress), which means that we do not see it as God sees it. I have even caught myself thinking at times that if I had been entrusted with the job of creating man and directing the destinies of the human race, I, in all modesty, would have done a better job, and, safeguarding of course man's freedom and allowing for a sufficient share of inevitable hardships, would have organized a happier world without much difficulty and to everybody's fair satisfaction. That is criticism of creation, which is, in the last analysis, lack of faith. I look at a person I think I know well, and tell myself wistfully: "Pity of a man. He could have done something if he had wanted to, but he has wasted his talents and ruined his life." Then I hear God say of the same person: "I have made him. He is my beloved son. I stand by him." My view does not coincide with God's view. My faith has still to grow.

Once I watched an interesting TV programme. Well, not interesting in itself, in fact it was absolutely boring as most such programmes are, but it became interesting for me when I realized the real lesson the programme was teaching me, quite different from anything intended by the producer. A television team had scoured the countryside stopping people in the streets, throwing the microphone in their teeth while the cameras recorded their faces, and asking them to say in exactly two minutes whatever they wanted to say for the whole country to hear and to see in a mass-contact programme. Two minutes do not give much scope for

13

imaginative rhetoric, and the hurried interviews soon degenerated into a monotonous review of strained faces and high-pitched voices. But then one common feature sprung up from the repetitious dullness of the improvised interviews, and I mentally grabbed it, held it before my mind and tested it against all the remaining protagonists of that uninspired evening for an hour that loomed like two. The common feature was this: every one of all the men and women interviewed, and there were close to thirty of them in the full-hour programme, every one without a single exception made use of his or her two minutes to voice a complaint. They were all different people in age, background, education, occupation, and they had quite different things to say in different words and different idiom, but the one thing they all agreed on was this: they all complained. A man in a village complained that there was no proper drainage in his place; another complained of the taxes he had to pay; many complained of the high cost of living; a schoolboy complained of the way he had been scolded by his father because he had failed in an examination, and tearfully pleaded with parents not to punish their children if they failed: that was a touching moment in the programme, the only redeeming instant in the long recital. The fact remained that all the participants in the programme chose to complain of something or other. They seemed to have thought to themselves: this is my chance; the whole country is watching and I have two minutes now, the only two minutes of my life when I can be seen and heard by thousands of people in the whole country; what shall I do in those two minutes? how shall I use them best? I know: I'll let go on something that really affects me..., yes, I'll complain; I'll say something against somebody or against something, and everybody will hear, and all will know what is wrong with the world. Indeed. Nobody thought of saying what is right with the world; nobody thought of relaxedly smiling into the camera and saying that he was happy, or of thanking people and expressing satisfaction and bringing two minutes of light into a dreary evening. Nobody. I watched steadily for the whole hour, and came away with the ominous conviction that we are a race of grumblers.

There is a little phrase which, in its own confidential linguistic message, gives us away and, whenever we use it, proclaims to the four winds our inborn capacity to complain. When someone is getting on fine in life, and we ask him how he is doing, he answers with a gesture of resignation: "Well, I can't complain." Poor man, he cannot complain! What a pity! He is longing to do it, longing to find something or somebody that could give him occasion to complain, but unfortunately everything is well with him, and he cannot afford the luxury of complaining. Though his very tone and gesture are already a clear complaint, that is, he is complaining that he cannot complain. At the end he has his way, after all.

We thrive on grievances. The first requirement in any registered establishment is a complaint box clearly visible — with the name occasionally softened to "suggestion box". In a small out-of-the-way railway station I passed through once, the first thing that caught my eye in the deserted platform was a notice in big red letters against the white wall, which proclaimed to a non-existing public its essential message: "Complaint book available." There was hardly any traffic, there were no timetables or notices, no restaurant or even waiting-room in the elementary railway station. But there was a complaint book. That was a status symbol more important than ten platforms and whirling public and rushing trains and steaming engines. A self-respecting railway station must have a complaint book, if it has nothing else. A wicked

15

thought crossed my mind: If there were no complaint book, where could I complain that there was no complaint book?

In God's universe there is no place for a complaint book. Grumbling is lack of faith. The sin against creation. Being wiser than God. Improving on his work. No wonder it draws from him a strong reaction and, in biblical language, causes his fire to burn. "There came a time when the people complained to the Lord of their hardships. When he heard, he became angry, and fire from the Lord broke out among them, and was raging at one end of the camp, when the people appealed to Moses. He interceded with the Lord, and the fire died down. Then they named that place Taberah (Burning), because the fire of the Lord had burned among them there." (Nm 11:1-3). That, and similar punishments, left their mark in Hebrew memory, and Paul reminded his correspondents of it: "Do not grumble against God, as some of your ancestors did... and were destroyed." (1 Cor 10:10). Grumbling destroys us because it sets us against reality, it is truly "kicking against the goad" which can only hurt the foot that kicks. When we grumble we dissociate ourselves from the course of events as arranged by God, we come out of the current of grace that runs through man's history, we isolate ourselves, we cut ourselves off, we shipwreck ourselves on the barren island of our own conceit to our own loss and suffering. Jesus exhorted us to not to judge our fellow men, and we not only break his commandment but, in our insolence, rise in judgement against God himself whose management of world affairs we disparage and criticize. We are harder on God's work than an art critic on the work of an immature artist. No wonder the fire burns.

On the contrary, by faith we place ourselves in the very perspective of God's will, and through it we enter the realm of peace and wisdom that it opens generously before us. God's will is what actually happens (I know of no better definition), and so by accepting what actually happens we fall in line with God's will, acknowledge his dominion and share his view. This brings peace and unity to the soul, reconciles the mind with the events of life, and sets the heart at rest among the vicissitudes of existence. This is no invitation to laziness or conformism, but the insistence to start action from the perspective of faith rather than from the calculations of man. Faith heals, as it removes inner resistance, protest, dissatisfaction with things around and therefore with oneself. No healthier climate can be devised for the soul, for life and for action, than that provided by a conscious, deep, final, trusting, faithful, total surrender into the hands of reality, which are the hands of God. The child sleeping contentedly in his mother's arms—knowing that from there he will wake up to movement and to life when the moment comes. That is the end of anxiety, of worries, of tensions, of the teasing gap between expectation and achievement, which weighs down the mind and stifles existence. The dogma of Divine Providence, apart from being good theology, is also good therapy. "I do not understand," said good old Father La Puente, forgotten classic of the art of contemplation, "I do not understand how a person who has true faith in God can ever be worried, anxious or agitated in his mind about anything; just as I do not understand either how a person who does not believe in God can even for a moment be free from fear, doubt and anxiety, as the success of his actions is certainly not in his hands, neither, for him, in the hands of a provident God who would order things wisely and lovingly for his greater good. Man, left to himself, is a helpless prey to worry." The man who spoke like that was a master of contemplation, and that circumstance explains the firmness of his statement

17

and shows the way to acquire a similar conviction. The way is prayer, meditation, contemplation. To have faith is to see things the way God sees them, and to see things the way God sees them it is essential to consult God, to spend time with him, to seek his company, to listen to his counsel, to search the Scriptures, to discern his will, to walk with him, to live with him. That, and nothing else, is prayer. Prayer, long, repeated, lasting, contemplative prayer is the climate where faith grows, where the "divine eye" is opened and a new perspective is obtained. Faith is born in prayer.

Another reflexion from Tagore in his prayer talks at Santiniketan. This world is like a large factory in which men toil day and night through a long life of bonded labour. A worker sweats for hours on end at his machine, mindful only of turning the right knobs and pulling the right levers so that no accident happens and he gets his salary at the end of the week, but he derives no joy from his work, understands nothing of what he is doing, and just operates his machine mechanically, himself almost a machine in the large workshop of the inhuman factory. Do you want to redeem yourself, asks Tagore, to escape the drudgery of the daily work, to save yourself from becoming a machine yourself in the machine world you live in, and to become truly a person, a man in dignity and freedom? Then just do one thing. Do work your shift at the factory with attention and care, do your duty and fill your time and mind your work; but then at the end of the day, when your turn is over and you leave your place and come out, do just one thing. As you come out of your daily tribulation, remove your clothes, heavy with grease and dirt and sweat, take a bath to make your mind holy and your body clean, and then change into fresh clothes and go up to the upper story of the factory building where you know the offices are, and there find your way into the chief manager's office, and knock and go in and sit…, and learn from him in leisurely conversation what the purpose of this factory is, its usefulness, its progress, what finished products are manufactured here, what their value is and what their markets are, how your concrete work at your machine fits into the general plan, and how your contribution helps in the final result. Meet the boss, talk with him, get his point of view, learn his plans, understand his purpose. Humanize yourself, that is, divinize yourself. Your work will continue, of course, because life has to be lived and production has to go on, but instead of being a cog in a machine, you will now be a partner in confidence, with a new outlook and a new spirit. Meet the boss, meet him often and trustingly and intimately, and your life will change even if your work does not.

That is Tagore's friendly advice. Meet the boss. Take time out from the daily business of living, wash and change clothes, go upstairs and meet the chief quietly in his office. That is prayer. That is where a new view is acquired and life is redeemed and strength is obtained for a new day. Faith is God's gift to the soul, and is to be nurtured in the contact with him which is daily prayer. Faith is God's view of things, and to preserve it we must frequent God's company in loving contemplation. Our faith is what our prayer life is.

WHICH SIDE IS WINNING?

"Faith is believing that the Kingdom has come, in spite of all appearances to the contrary." That definition by Joachim Jeremias almost matches the Irishman's definition: "Faith is believing what the Church says, in spite of knowing it is not true." There is humour and mischief in that saying, as there is in the jolly limmerick that expresses with seemingly inconsequential irresponsibility the heart of the trial to which the religious intellect is subject while on earth:

"God made a most hopeful beginning,
and man later spoiled it by sinning.
We know that the story
will end in God's glory;
but at present the other side's winning!"

Faith is the bridge that spans the credibility gap between what is and what should be, what our eyes see and what our hearts believe, between present and future, between heaven and earth. "Faith is the assurance of our hope, the proof of the things we do not see." (Hb 11:1). And "hope would not be hope at all if its objects were in view; how could a man

21

still hope for something which he sees? And if we are hoping for something still unseen, then we need endurance to wait for it." (Rm 8:24). Faith and hope are a leap into the unknown, and therein lies their difficulty—and their worth. To step out into darkness holding the hand of a friend is an act of trust in that friend. When that friend is God, the action becomes religion, and man earns heaven.

I did go through that little exercise once during a sensitivity session with a group of friends. Choose a partner. Let him (in this case, her) blindfold you. Then hold her hand and allow yourself to be led wherever she wants. Not a word to be spoken. Just keep a mental record of what is happening to you in the inside as you go along. And after the blind walk, tell your partner before the group all that you have been experiencing while in darkness. Fear? suspicion? apprehension? Were you relaxed or tense or amused? Did you find the experience long or short, pleasant or annoying? How did your feelings towards your partner change in the process? What have you learned? Our whole life is a long blind walk holding the hand of God. We shall have a lot to tell him when the blindfold is removed at the end of the walk.

The walk is an apt metaphor, because faith is not just intellectual believing but subsequent acting. To believe that the Kingdom has come is to live in the Kingdom, under its laws and with its citizenship, even if that makes us appear as strangers in a world that does not acknowledge the existence of the Kingdom. We are the true citizens, yet we appear as aliens, and the inner tension our souls experience between the appearance of things and the reality of grace is proyected into the outside tension to act as citizens of heaven while still very much on earth.

During one of the unfortunate wars between India and Pakistan, an Indian army officer was captured and kept incommunicado in Karachi till the end of the war, when he was set free, came back to India and told his experience. During his captivity, he said, he was allowed to read newspapers and listen to the radio, but, of course, only Pakistani newspapers and radio stations. Accordingly he heard and read day by day news of the war which said repeatedly that India was losing on all fronts, and was about to be defeated. That was all the information he had. And yet, as he himself told when he was free in India recollecting his past captivity, he refused to believe even then that his country was losing, and was sure in his heart, in spite of all the constant propaganda to the contrary, that India was winning the war all along. And that was the fact. India was winning, and in a few days obtained the final victory that forced the peace. The experience of that gallant officer, when I read it in the press, gave me an example of how faith works in us... if only we too are proud of our heavenly citizenship, and gallant patriots of the Kingdom. All the information we receive is adverse and contrary to our beliefs. The Enemy is winning. Honesty does not pay, to tell the truth only creates problems, violence always gets the upper hand, and goodness has no place left in this troubled world. Those are the news we read and hear day by day and hour by hour. The Kingdom is being defeated, and there is no hope of victory. And yet, in our heart of hearts, we know that that is not true. In spite of all the enemy propaganda we know deep down in our conscience that the Kingdom is winning, that truth prevails, that honesty pays, and Jesus is King. This is heavenly patriotism, which is divine faith. Let us wait in joyful patience for the final news, and when victory comes we will tell our experience.

23

We do in fact live our faith already in many ways, and it is on that happy conviction and practice that we have to build high and strong in order to let our faith reach its full measure in our lives. Every day we perform an exalted act of faith as we attend and participate in the Eucharist. Routine takes its toll unavoidably even in this holiest of actions, but for all our imperfections, distractions and hesitations, we rise to a daily height of pure faith when we gather round the altar and listen to God's word in reverence, greet each other like brothers, and bend in adoration before the living Christ while our hands touch humble bread and our lips sing hymns of joy into the open windows to tell an indifferent world that we believe in hope and are committed to love in the name of him who loves us all and is present here in truth and sacrament in our midst. Our daily Eucharist is a summit of faith, and the realisation of it can go a long way to lift the whole day into the realm of grace and the perspective of faith in which it is meant to unfold itself.

We do not seem to find it easy, however, to transfer the atmosphere of faith of those hallowed moments to the rest of the day, and to recognize God, his word and his will as easily in surrounding events as we do in the sacramental rite. We, who readily find in ourselves faith enough to say that what appears to be bread and wine is in reality Jesus and God—no mean achievement of grace in our souls—do not find it so easy to say that what appears to us to be harmful in life is indeed beneficial, and what appears as loss is gain. We recognize God in bread and wine, but we do not recognize him so easily in storm and wind, in the rain that drenches us or the accident that cripples us, in social problems or in domestic trials, in daily events or in world crises. And yet the situation is similar: the contrast between appearances and reality, between the surface and the depth, the tasteless bread and the living Christ. God under a veil, be it of food and drink or of news and events. True faith reaches up to him through any circumstances. The idea comes from Père de Caussade in an inspired page. "Does not reason, as well as faith, reveal to us the real presence of the divine love in all creatures and in all the events of life as undubitably as the word of Jesus Christ and the Church reveal to us the presence of the sacred flesh of our Saviour under the Eucharistic species? Do we not know that by all these creatures and all these events, the divine Love desires to unite himself to us, that he has produced, ordained or permitted everything that surrounds us or happens to us in view of this union, the sole end of all his designs; that he uses, to attain this end, the worst as well as the best of creatures and the most disagreable as well as the pleasantest events, and that the more naturally repellent the means of that union, the more meritorious it becomes? But if all this is true, why should not every moment of our lives be a sort of communion with divine love continuously producing in our souls the fruits of that communion in which we receive the body and blood of the Son of God? The latter, truly, has a sacramental efficacy lacking to the former, but on the other hand how much more frequently the former can be renewed and how greatly can its merit grow through the perfection of the dispositions in which it is performed. How true that the holiest life is mysterious in its simplicity and its apparent humble state. Divine banquet, perpetual festival.... God ever given and received under appearances of the greatest weakness and nothingness! God chooses what is blame-worthy to the natural judgement and what human prudence leaves on one side. Of all things God makes mysteries and sacraments of love, and gives himself to souls to the full extent of their faith through the very medium which might appear to injure them."

Another parallel by the same master is between the word of God as it reaches us through the Scriptures and through the daily vicissitudes of our lives. I summarize his thought. God speaks to men in general through sundry events of history, through discoveries and achievements as well as through revolutions and war; and he speaks to concrete persons through the detailed happenings of their day-to-day life. But instead of hearing his voice, most men see in such circumstances only the play of human factors, power and success, envy and bad luck, all mixed by blind chance and willful malice on the part of men, and so they find fault with all that happens, quarrel with facts and rebel against their lot. Those same men, at least the devout believers among them, respect the Scriptures as God's word, and would not dream of tampering with them or imposing their own sense on them. If, then, they recognize God's voice in the inspired Scriptures, why do they not recognize it too in the happenings that affect their life, when it is the same voice that speaks? God's will appears in the words he speaks from moment to moment, in the course of events and through whatever happens to us and around us, as much as it appears in the words of Holy Scripture; in fact it can be said that the Holy Spirit continues to write a new Gospel with our lives and actions; "Jesus Christ is the same yesterday, today and for ever", his life continues in us, and the living Gospel we make up is being written under the same inspiration. "What a fine book the Holy Spirit is writing now! The book is in the press, there is no day on which the letters which make it up are not being composed, on which the ink is not applied and the sheets printed. But we dwell in the night of faith; the paper is blacker than the ink, the characters are all in confusion, the language is not of this world, nothing can be understood of it. You will be able to read this book only in heaven. If we could see the life of God

26

and could contemplate all creatures, not in themselves, but in their principle, if we could also see the life of God in all objects, how his divine action moves them, mingles them, assembles them, opposes them to each other, pushes them all to the same point by diverse means, we should recognize that all things in this divine work have their reasons, their scale of measurement, their mutual relations. Teach me, Divine Spirit, to read in this book of life!"

If faith walks in darkness (and that is its risk), it walks holding God's hand (and that is its strength). There is no greater power on earth, no stronger motivation nor firmer support than the power of religious faith. Men and women through all ages have given up their lives cheerfully on its strength, have lived in deserts and caves, have kept virginity and served the destitute, have prayed and toiled with heroic perseverance in the holiest of causes. The epistle to the Hebrews weaves an inspired summary of the history of salvation from creation to the prophets on the single thread of faith, since "it is for their faith that the men of old stand on record." (Hb 11:2). A man's faith is the measure of his life, of his achievements in it, of the joy he lives with and the imprint he leaves on the world. Man is as large—or as small— as his faith.

I have said religious faith. There is a kind of secular faith, of belief in oneself or one's stars or one's destiny or one's luck, often appealed to and made the basis of success in life, of why some forge ahead and some are left behind, and such psychological faith does play a part in man's behaviour, although on a quite different level. Vergil's oarmen are the example of that faith in themselves that makes them give of their best and win the race: *"possunt quia posse videntur."* "They do it because they believe they can do it." Confidence in oneself is essential to success, and,

27

negatively, if I do not think I can possibly win the race, and I enter it in a despondent mood, I am not likely to get the prize. It is important to believe in oneself in order to achieve anything in life, and the point I want to make here is that the best way, and indeed in the long run the only way to believe deeply and firmly in myself, is to believe in God as my Father and Lord, who loves me and wants me to lead a happy and useful life in the world he has created. The only true basis for the "I can do all things" is, with St. Paul, the sequel to "in him who strengthens me" (Phil 4:13). Religious faith is the only sure foundation of psychological faith. A mere pep talk, a friendly "cheer up!" or "best of luck!" even if accompanied by gentle strokes on the victim's back cannot have a lasting effect in the midst of adverse circumstances or looming trials. True faith is something much deeper than an empty "trusting one's stars" or enjoying a "spell of good luck". One may win a boat race on it, like Vergil's oarmen, but not the race of life.

Faith in oneself can, subtly and dangerously, tend to replace faith in God, and has done so in history and continues to do so in practice. That deviation is important, and I want to analyse it now.

THE ELEPHANT AND THE CROCODILE

I have sung lustily in church in younger days songs of penance and resolve like the following: "Jesus, my Lord, behold at length the time/when I resolve to turn away from crime." And I have drawn much spiritual strength and comfort from such devotional hymns through many years. Today I look at them and at the attitude they created in me together with the whole spirituality they represented, and I find something in it not altogether healthy and balanced, and rather far from my present understanding of the realities of the soul. Just look at the words: "Behold the time... when I resolve...". Jesus is told, reverently and well-meaningly to be sure, but, so I think, rather misguidedly, to stand back and watch with interest while I on my own, of my own resolve and on my own steam, turn away from whatever evil I was doing, and embark upon a holy life from now on. I am exaggerating for clarity, but the point is there. It is my resolve, my determination, my willpower, my energies that effect my repentance and move me to act and see me through in my good purpose. It is my effort that saves me. That is the whole trend of the spirituality reflected in that song. And a rather unfortunate trend it is.

A better example, both for the quality of the verse and for the depth of its feeling, is the beautiful poem:

"It matters not how strait the gate,
how charged with punishments the scroll;
I am the master of my fate,
I am the captain of my soul."

There is strength and charm in those verses, all the more remarkable as they came from a poet who was an invalid from childhood; but again, as an attitude to life and to virtue in the face of God's grace, such a stand, though common enough in practice, is misguided and harmful. "I am the captain of my soul." I run my life and fight my battles and win my victories. I do it. God, of course, is kind enough to watch my exploits and bless them from on high, but the credit for them is fundamentally mine. I make my own life. I run my show.

It is lawful, no doubt, and even beneficial at times to stress man's responsibility and freedom in handling his life; but if that attitude leads, as it only too often does in practice, to effectively cancelling, minimizing, forgetting the essential role that the divine action and God's supreme dominion play in the soul, that would amount to denying grace and suppressing faith. The balance between man's freedom and God's grace is delicate, and man tends to tip the scales his side—to his own undoing.

This tendency has a name and a history. The time was the fifth century, and the name Pelagius. That learned monk was of the opinion that original sin does not exist, and, in consequence, man effects his own salvation by himself, independently of God's grace. He was promptly branded a heretic, and his doctrine, Pelagianism, duly condemned.

Now Pelagius is long dead, but Pelagianism is not. We are all secret followers of the ancient sect, if not in conscious theory, certainly in actual practice. We believe that it is our effort that fundamentally and eventually counts in our spiritual lives, and we minimize in practice the essential, salvific, vivifying action of God in each moment of our existence and in each decision of our will. Pelagianism is the greatest enemy of a life of faith, and we are all Pelagians at heart. We are and want to be independent, self-reliant, self-sufficient. We do pray for God's grace and thank him for his help, but a long, systematic, ascetical training has focussed our view excessively, almost exclusively, on our own will, and to it we attribute, in the last instance, the result of our endeavours. While God's praise is on our lips, our heart is filled with self-satisfaction at our achievements, and even when we do not quite succeed in spiritual endeavours we inwardly tell ourselves that we have not succeeded because we have not really tried, and we know that if we really want we can surely do better—with God's help, of course, as an afterthought. The point is important and delicate, and I want to clarify it.

I know I do not pray very well these days, and in self-examination I tell myself something like this (someone has remarked that whatever we "tell ourselves" is always a lie, and this case certainly fits the pattern): It is true that my prayer nowadays is not exactly what it could be, but then it is also true that I am not giving myself a chance. I am not at my best right now. I am too busy, too tired, too worried about a thousand things; I come to prayer, when I come at all, with a burdened mind and an unsettled spirit, I come in a hurry, between business, at odd times and without any preparation. No wonder my prayer is lousy, and my contemplation non-existent. But I also know that if I take myself in hand, if I put

31

my mind to it as I know I can do when I mean it, if I take time out and find a quiet place, if I read a spiritual book at night and go to bed in time and rise early and seek solitude and seat in lotus posture on a thick prayer rug and close my eyes and concentrate my mind and still my heart and think of holy things..., I know that if I do all that I can pray like an angel, and let the whole heavenly court watch my performance. I will not disappoint them. I certainly can do it if I mean to do it. Only now I am not really trying. If I put only half as much interest in my prayer life as I put in my business or in my work, if I prepare my prayer as I prepare my public speeches or my lectures or my business meetings or my trips, if I were to seek success in prayer with the determination with which I seek success in life, I would certainly obtain it. Oh, I could really become a saint if I set my heart on it; only I never quite make up my mind, and somehow let myself remain in my present mediocrity; but if I really wanted...!

The paragraph I have just written is perfectly realistic, and in fact it faithfully reflects the way I myself have felt often in past years, and the way I have seen many spiritual people feel when speaking to me of their difficulties in prayer and in the life of the spirit in general. And yet that paragraph could have been signed by Pelagius in person. It is a neat statement of pure heresy. For less than that were people burnt at the stake in hardier days! I do and I get and I achieve, and if I have not more to show for it as present, it is because I am not exerting myself fully. God is just forgotten, and spiritual advancement is conditioned solely to my own efforts—or lack of them. I hasten to say that, naturally, I do count on God, and since his help is always forthcoming, it will be there in any case, available whenever I need it, and so I had not mentioned it. God has been taken for granted; in other words, he is ignored. Man alone counts.

32

The true attitude taught by the Gospels is the opposite one. We are asked to do all that is in our power, and then to add: "We are useless servants." One man sows and another waters, but "it is God that gives the growing." Our sowing and watering is certainly required, but the growth comes from God. Every single one of my actions is inextricably mine and his; his grace and my freedom are woven into a unique act; his initiative and my cooperation are one single movement of human existence in divine hands. The balance is so fine that one or the other of the extremes is bound to be now and then stressed to the detriment of the other, and it has happened so in history. Man's freedom has been at times overshadowed by God's power (if God does all that I do, how am I free? If God knows all that I am going to do, how can I do otherwise?), and God's influence has been minimized also at times under man's moral franchise (if I am fully responsible for my actions, how does God come in there?). In our days the latter is the favourite heresy.

I not only profess genuine admiration for Buddhism but also feel personal gratitude towards it as I have profited considerably in my own life by its doctrines and practices. I, however, find myself miles away from the basic attitude of Buddhism that makes man's personal unremitting effort the exclusive condition for ultimate liberation. The Buddha's own vow is forbidding in its suprahuman determination: "Though only my skin, sinews and bones remain, and my blood and flesh dry up and wither away, yet never from this seat will I stir until I have attained full enlightenment." And Zen, for all its charming wisdom and winning common sense, requires even today a similar attitude from its unconditional followers: "The central theme of Zen is sustained self-effort, for in the last analysis one is liberated not by his fellows, not by the roshi, not even by the Buddha,

33

and certainly not by any supernatural being, but by one's own unfaltering, indefatigable exertions." Those are words to gladden Pelagius' heart. It is clear that they ignore God and preclude faith in him. I bring them here, quoted from a serious Zen manual, to show the logical extreme to which the exaggerated stress on man's role in salvation must lead. To see the ultimate expression of this attitude in others can help us to discern its beginnings in ourselves. Pelagius, after all, was a Christian monk.

I even dare, with full reverence for persons, and full allowance for the influence of the age one lives in, and of training and tradition and idiosyncrasies, as well as for possible misunderstanding on my part, to point out some attitudes in saints whom I have regarded as models for a period of my life, and who now, in those attitudes, appear to me to be less imitable. St. John Berchmans expressed in his maxims with linguistic vehemence his famous outburst *"disrumpar potius"*, his heroic resolve "to burst open rather than transgress even once the smallest rule of the Society of Jesus". Generous proposal, to be sure, but rather unrealistic given the complexity of the said rules, and the weakness of human nature when even the just man, according to Scripture, "falls seven times a day". To a disciple who was pledging his allegiance for ever with similar emphasis, Jesus said sadly: "Before the cock crows, you'll disown me thrice." I admire the youthful enthusiasm of the canonized patron of Jesuit youth, while I doubt his wisdom in this. St. Aloysius Gonzaga, another model of youth, reportedly made a vow to spend daily one continuous hour of morning prayer without any distraction, so that if he became aware of any distraction during prayer, he would start the prayer again, and repeat the new start as many times as necessary till he obtained sixty clear continuous minutes of distractionless

34

prayer. One of his biographers observed, with a better sense of humour, that all his hero got from that resolution was a headache. Willpower alone is no way to prayer.

Father Roothaan, outstanding commentator of Ignatian spirituality, is of the opinion that one of the reasons for the practical failure, often reported, of a method so simple and effective as Ignatius' "particular examen" is precisely its efficiency. The paradox has an easy explanation, and concerns me here. The practice of the particular examen calls for focussing on a concrete personal defect to be eradicated, and applying to it singleheartedly a systematic method of elimination. First thing in the morning "on getting up" is to bring to mind the offending habit and to renew the determination to exterminate it. During the day, whenever a lapse is recorded, the person is to put his hand on his breast as a physical gesture to mark the fall (almost as a cross to mark the spot of an accident) and to register it in the victim's memory. Twice in the day, at noon and at night, time is to be taken to recall the day hour by hour, and to score the failures, marking on a straight line the points for the morning, and in a lower parallel line those for the evening. The next day the procedure is repeated, and the scores are compared. Ignatius does even something quite out of character with him and which he never again does in all his writings: he provides a diagram. He writes seven "g's", one below the other, the first one, big, for Sunday, and the remaining six for the other week days. The mystery of the "g" seems to be that it stands in Spanish for *"gula"* (gluttony), as the first vice he feared existed and wanted eliminated in his followers. Then from each "g" two horizontal lines jut out, waiting for the points of the day to be scored on them. The interesting point of the diagram is that the lines of each day are slightly shorter than those of the previous day, providing thus a kind of inverted staircase. Ignatius was so optimistic about the outcome of his method that he felt sure the failures would diminish day by day, and shorter lines would suffice at each scoring!

Too optimistic in fact, thinks Roothaan. And he sees the weakness of the method in its very strength. The procedure is so clear, so pointed, so efficiently enlisting all the powers of the soul and bringing them to bear on a single concrete conquerable objective, that the vice in question seems doomed to extinction from the start. Gluttony does not stand a chance. If I single out a defect I want to correct in myself, think of it each day first thing in the morning and last thing at night, beat my breast at each slip, keep accounts twice a day, renew my resolve, check progress, pursue with relentless determination my singleminded goal, and do not yield till I see it conquered—I feel absolutely sure that in the end I shall overcome whatever I set out to overcome. That is the trouble, says Roothaan. Too efficient. It almost works by itself. It can create the impression (though this was far from Ignatius' mind) that one can succeed by the sheer efficacy of the method, without any reference to God or grace. Ignatius, to be sure, provides such reference, but it can be overlooked, and the method used as a device efficient in itself. In fact a perfectly similar method was used and recommended by Benjamin Franklin as a purely secular tool for self-improvement. That is its danger, says Roothaan, and that is where it breaks down in practice. It becomes purely a willpower exercise, a programmed procedure, a Pelagian practice. And it fails. The lines do not become shorter. The defect does not go. The expectation is not fulfilled. Apart from grace no vice can be conquered. Not even gluttony.

The experience I had as a young aspirant to sanctity

36

was in a way similar to that. I read in "The Imitation of Christ": "If only we uprooted one vice every year, we would soon become perfect." That appealed to me in my naively Pelagian frame of mind. That was pure algebra. I had only to catalogue my vices, which were anyhow everybody's vices, and so I could just take them down from any spirituality manual or from any of those handy lists of human weaknesses for ready examination of conscience available in any prayer book. and arrange them in alphabetical order for a systematic attack. The list would be finite in any case. and it could be reduced to a manageable number of heads. Then there would only be a question of taking one by one the offending habits, applying to each in turn the powerful "particular examen", and getting them out one at a time without further ado. No vicious habit, however ingrained in my behaviour, could possibly resist the concerted effort of all my ascetical batteries for one year. I would feel offended if anybody would doubt that. I saw myself ticking off the exiting vices as they left my company year by year, and calculating on an approximation the time left for me to attain perfection. In so many years I would be a saint. It was to be just a matter of time and willpower. And therefore it never was. The algebra did not work. Virtue cannot be programmed. Grace cannot be ignored. Much later in life I came to know a very holy old priest who told me one day with a confidentiality that was unusual in him: "I spent half of my life making resolutions—and breaking them. Now I'm making up in the second half of my life. I haven't made any resolution for years, and I'll never make one again. When I see something in me which would need improvement. I now point it out to God in prayer. My approach has changed."

That change of approach is the right attitude to spiritual growth. and in saying "change" I am aware that I imply there must be first a period of "Pelagianism" in our life, a period of stress on our own effort and determination, from which we later are to change into another period of greater emphasis on God's action on the soul. That is normally the case, and that is as it should be. Avoiding extremes either way, it is beneficial to begin life with a stress on one's own action, responsibility, personal endeavour and observable achievements. The young man, to be moved into action, needs to feel his own muscle and taste his own victories. He is to be presented with a concrete goal he can obtain, with a mountain peak he can climb, and he will set out and strain every nerve and brave every obstacle and do great things and fill his heart with his triumph. A young man has to believe that the moon is within reach, that men can actually change, that society can improve and mankind can become wise. And then he must be left to feel, at least for a time, that his efforts count for everything, that he is the main actor, that he is an achiever, that all depends on him, and that his plans and his ideas and his endeavours are sure to make a difference to the welfare of the human race and to the future of mankind. Achievement, willpower, energy, efficiency are values he must cherish and results he must experience. To get going, even in the spiritual life, to shake off laziness and overcome indifference, to enter the discipline of prayer, the path of virtue, the habit of self-denial, the seriousness of a commitment for life, a young man has to be given an incentive, an attraction, a prize, he has to feel that the work is his and the success his victory, he has to taste the reward of being able to sense and to say that he is running his own race and living his own life. In a word, he has to be for a time, and without knowing it himself, a genuine Pelagian.

A wise friend of mine liked to illustrate this point with a personal story, or maybe it was just a parable. Once, he said,

The Elephant and the Crocodile

I was sitting in a railway compartment waiting for the train to start, and a small child was in the same compartment asking questions as children do. He asked: "When will the train start?" I saw my chance, and volunteered to answer his question. I said: "The train will start when we start pushing. Unless we push, how can it start?" The child opened his big eyes in surprise. "Really?"—"Of course."—"Unless we push it doesn't start?"—"It cannot. Once we start, it will go by itself, but to start we must push."—"Then let us push."— "Yes, only just wait for all passengers to come in. I'll tell you when to push." I kept an eye on the station clock to check the exact time. I watched the red light turn to amber, I heard the station-master's whistle, and then I shouted to the boy, "Now! Push for all you're worth!" Then he and I started pushing with all our strength on the wood panel of the compartment towards the engine. The boy pushed and pushed, and soon a contented smile curled his lips and lit his face. The train was moving! Very slowly at first, then little by little gaining speed, and soon at full steam with the rhythmical panting of the brave engine. I congratulated the boy on his pushing. "We did it! Wasn't that great!" He looked immensely pleased. He was travelling in a train he had helped to start. Such a feeling cannot fail to give satisfaction. To tell him that the engine was running on coal would have spoiled his fun and dampened his spirits. He will have plenty of time in life to find out.

It is good for man, it is the right course of things, it is providential that he starts in life with youthful enthusiasm, that he believes himself to be the hero, that he thinks the train starts to move because he pushes it. That will make him push and work and toil, and will bring out the best in him. All that is necessary for a start. The tragedy comes when that attitude, which is fine for the beginning of the spiritual life,

39

stays and continues and perpetuates itself, and the man keeps pushing the train through life as though he were a child. The novice, through examinations of conscience and resolutions and exhortations and pressure of his peers and superiors and circumstances, begins striving for personal holiness as a hard-working student for a first class in an examination, or a junior executive doing extra time to obtain a quick promotion. The beginning is fine, but the problem is that this attitude of a spiritual over-achiever may become habit with the novice and stick to him for life. That is unfortunate, because such an attitude is suitable only for a launching, and if continued indefinitely will soon generate dissatisfaction, frustration and despair, with the temptation to give it all up, as repeated efforts do not seem now to bear fruit. Trains do not move when we push them.

I define the practical attitude as I understand it. First, try with all your might, never quite forgetting God, of course, but as though in practice you were going to achieve perfection all by yourself, and believe for a time that this is being so. Then, and this "then" will take years, come round, review your experience, be honest and admit to yourself that you are getting nowhere, that perfection looks farther away than when you started, that you are not a saint and not likely to become one, that you pray worse than when you started and experience more distractions and temptations than ever; and turn to God acknowledging that it is only from his mercy and grace that you can expect help to advance and to conquer. Unless you have tried your best and failed, you can never be humble, because you will keep thinking at the back of your mind that if you had tried harder you would have succeeded. Try then your best by all means, see the futility of your own efforts by themselves, admit defeat, and now come to God, surrender to him and open yourself wholeheartedly to his action in you. Faith will now fertilize your efforts. and your life will fructify. You are in good hands.

A story from Hindu mythology. Indra's elephant, Gajendra, had gone to take a bath in the river. The elephant is the symbol of power and strength, and therefore of self-reliance when it comes to pulling or pushing or fighting or making his way through anywhere. He does not need anybody's help to hold his own in any place in the forest, in any circumstance in life. He is fearless and independent. Yet this time Gajendra was in trouble. A crocodile in the river had come up and attached itself to his leg, and then was pulling him into the current and the deep waters. The elephant pulled back, but to no avail. The water was not his kingdom, his feet slipped in the mud, and the crocodile's teeth sinking into his sensitive flesh dazed his brains and blurred his sight. Yet Gajendra pulled and pulled, he wanted to save his life, his prestige, his position as the strongest inhabitant of the jungle. He certainly could do it as he had always done it; it was only a matter of gathering all his strength together and pulling with all his might. He did so—and lost more ground. Seeing that he was soon going to disappear under water, he desperately changed his tactics. He thought of God and prayed, as even elephants can pray in legends to be an example to man: "My own strength has not been able to save me. I am going under. Help me!" And in that very instant Vishnu appeared on his eagle-mount Garuda, and saved Gajendra from the grip of the crocodile and from its own pride. Divine help appeared when the strongest being on earth accepted its own limitation. Parable of grace. God comes when man realizes his own limitation. When we give up our pride. we are ready for faith. It is then that real life begins.

THE LAW AND THE PROMISE

There are two key words to understand and describe our relationship to God in our desire to do his will and win his presence for ever. Both those words are in St. Paul and form the basis of his experience and his doctrine: the Law and the Promise. We shall find it worth our effort to follow his thought and mirror our experience in his.

The Law, in his terminology, is the bilateral contract between God and man, by which man binds himself to obey God's commandments (the "Law"), and God in return binds himself to protect man as his own. "You shall be my people, and I will be your God." A treaty with signatures, where each of the parties has to abide by the conditions stipulated in it, and if one of the parties fails to keep its part of the contract, the other is not bound any more by it. The prototype of such a relationship, veritable obsession in Paul's mind throughout his writings, is the Sinai pact between Yahweh and Israel, embodied in the Mosaic Law, from which Paul took his term: the Law. The people of Israel were to keep the rules of moral behaviour, social relations and divine cult as prescribed by Moses in the name of God,

43

and God, in his turn, took it upon himself to guide them through the desert, give them victory against all the adversaries they would meet on the way, and finally establish them in a beautiful and fertile land. Man keeps the commandments, and God grants him eternal life. A very businesslike arrangement that makes for clarity, security and mutual responsibility. It may be hard to keep the conditions, but man knows that if he does keep them, God will also unfailingly do his part of the bargain, and man's future will be guaranteed in this life and in the next. The catch with the system, and Paul never misses a chance to expose it and enlarge upon it with characteristic vehemence, is that man never will, never can, never does fulfill his part of the contract. Man sins, and the whole plan collapses. "There is no just man, not one; no one who understands, no one who seeks God. All have swerved aside, all alike have become debased...; no one can say anything in self defence...; no human being can be justified in the sight of God for having kept the Law. The Law brings only consciousness of sin." (Rm 3:10-20). The Law is a beautiful structure, but it does not work because man can never live up to it.

And here comes the Promise. In place of the Law of Moses, the Promise made now to Abraham "and his descendants", so that the heritage of the children of God "may not depend on the Law but on the Promise." (Gl 3:18). The Promise is free, unilateral, unconditional. God pledges his word on his own, promises his love, which is the highest guarantee of all welfare temporal and eternal, and invites man to enter the realm of grace as an adopted son in God's own family. All that man has to do, and a great deed that is in love and trust, is to believe that God's offer is true, to let God be God and rule supreme and bestow his blessing on him, without asking for written guarantees or demanding previous explanations. That is faith. In the bilateral contract there was not much room for it, as the setting was rather that of a business transaction where the fulfilment of a condition brought about by itself, in virtue of the existing document, the expected result from the other side. But here the Promise is unilateral; we have no claim, no contract, no written statement. We just believe that God will be as good as his word, that his love is eternal and his mercy without bounds, and we throw ourselves into his arms in loving confidence and total faith. We will certainly continue to do our best and lead a good life and help our neighbour and say our prayers, but the emphasis will not be on our efforts but on God's grace. We do not build up an uncontestable claim to heaven; we rather trust our Father and leave our future in his hands. That is the meaning of believing in him.

And now comes the interesting point. I have described the meaning of the Law and the Promise, with a bias towards the Promise, as Paul himself shows, and it would follow from the description that we should all obviously and naturally adopt the attitude implied in the theology of the Promise. And yet the fact is that in practice we do not. We prefer the Law to the Promise. We prefer the (apparent) security of a bilateral contract, we want to have a claim, a right, a proof, we want to bind God to admit us into heaven by presenting a document that entitles us to be admitted by virtue of the previous agreement; we want to build up a credit that will by itself ensure our everlasting happiness. We feel safer handling the business of our eternal salvation ourselves than leaving it in the hands of God; we want the certificate, the witnesses, the official stamp on our life story to show the pass at the gate and win admission. And so in practice we want a contract, we want a two-way agreement, we want the Law. And by now it will be clear, I hope, that the Law is Pelagianism, while the Promise is faith.

A charming young man, whom I once tried to influence into becoming a Jesuit, and who was too clever for me and never joined, showed me one day in confidence a holy picture he always carried on his person and never put aside wherever he went. It was a picture of the Sacred Heart, and when he turned it round and showed me the other side, I saw on it nine dates and a signature at the bottom of them with a rubber stamp on it. He explained to me: "These are the dates of the first Fridays of nine consecutive months on which I received holy communion to fulfil the condition set by the Sacred Heart himself when he revealed to St. Margaret Mary that those who did that would not die with sin on their souls; and below those dates is the signature of my parish priest to certify that I have fulfilled the condition, with the parish stamp on it. Now, this is the one piece of paper I want to have on me when I die, and that is why I always carry it with me. This is my ticket to heaven." He then kissed the picture reverently, and placed it carefully in his wallet, and the wallet in the breast pocket of his coat.

I have written a book on the Sacred Heart, of which I am proud, and I know the value and meaning of the devotion of the Nine Fridays. Popular devotions have their rightful place among the people of God, and many derive genuine profit from them. What concerns me here is not the First Fridays, but the picture, the dates, the signature, the rubber stamp, and the determined resolution of that fine young man to carry his talisman always on his person. He was leaving nothing to God, he did not even trust God's memory or St. Peter's good will at the gate, and he wanted the rubber stamp of the parish to prove, like a heavenly affidavit, that he was entitled to a holy death and a place in heaven. He would literally force his way into heaven. If ever there was a Law, a contract, an insurance policy, this was an example of it down to the very materiality of the paper and the witness and the rubber stamp. Nothing left to chance. I have a right, I have paid the premium, I can collect. And I will treasure this bit of paper as I treasure my very soul. The only point my young friend did not explain to me was how he was going to carry the paper through the clouds of heaven, as the soul has no pockets. He had not thought of it yet.

The attitude, if not the rubber stamp, is common among us, to the extent of being almost universal. Another example, also related to Fridays. I knew a holy woman who early in her religious life had taken the resolution to fast every Friday, eating nothing at all the whole day, and had faithfully kept it through many devoted years. Later in life, however, as her health deteriorated, she began to find it difficult to spend one whole day without any food, and the doctor advised against the fast. Yet she demurred. "For so many years", she said, "I have kept this resolution, not without some hardship; and if now at the end of my life I break it, I will lose all the merit I had acquired till now with its observance. I do not want to make void my previous penance. I prefer to suffer a little more for whatever years I may still live, and keep my claim valid before God." That was the contract again. I do my part, and you do yours. No idea of God's mercy, God's generosity, God's readiness to appreciate what she had done so far and to reward her for what she desired to do—even if she could not do it now. No trusting God, not leaving anything to God, but insisting stubbornly on keeping to the letter her part of the stipulated conditions so as not to lose her imagined rights. Her only worry was to keep her claim intact; her only attitude, to push her way in. The Law against the Promise.

Some years ago I published in Gujarati a book on the

parables of the Gospel. Most of my readers are Hindus, and they appreciate and like the message of Jesus, particularly as embodied in his masterly parables. In fact, I wrote the book at the request of a Hindu publisher, and I had full confidence it would go well with my readers. I, however, anticipated trouble in one parable—and my fears proved founded. The parable was the one of the owner of the vineyard who hires labourers at different times in the day from early morning to one hour before sunset when work in the fields comes to an end and wages are paid. Some work a whole worker's day in the scorching heat, while others put in only one hour's work under the last kindly rays of the setting sun. Yet, when wages are paid, all receive exactly the same, while the senior labourers protest in wrathful indignation — and so did my readers. That is not fair! God is unjust! If the man who works one hour is paid one denarius, the man who works eight has to be paid eight. As plain as that. No amount of explanations or theologies or considerations of any kind can get over that fact. I had taken pains in my book to explain that God is free and merciful, and so, while certainly giving at least the stipulated wages to all, can surely give more to some if he so chooses. But my arguments did not convince my readers, any more than the land-owner's explanations convinced his workers. One is one, and eight is eight, and there was no moving them from that. I gave up on my mail, and went to enlarge that chapter with further elaboration, and little hope of success, in the second edition of the book. The protest mail eventually subsided, as did the protests of the workers in the parable, not because people were convinced in either case, but because they eventually gave up.

That attitude, and it is not only that of my Hindu readers, but also that of my Christian brothers, is precisely and neatly the attitude of the Law. One for one, and eight for eight. The calculation, the contract, the exact amount. Work your time and claim your wages. And these, then, have to be paid exactly and equitably and openly. God is told what he has to do, and he is expected to do it. Man, in his calculating ways, will not allow God to be merciful, to be free, to do what he wants with his graces. Man will prefer the apparent security of a fixed contract to the open situation of trust in God's generosity. It is not precisely or chiefly jealousy against the favoured worker that makes the others protest, but rather the fact that by upsetting their calculations the master shatters their security, their safety, their hold on the situation. If God does not abide by the conditions set down on paper, who knows what he will do next? If the contract is not honoured, where do we stand? If he is so plainly unfair this time, how can we trust him the next? Man prefers the security of lower wages to the possibility of higher wages which he does not control. He prefers the Law to the Promise, effort to grace, and Pelagius to Paul. Man finds it difficult to live on faith.

Now, there is a curious historical fact which adds spice to this important theological truth. There was a rabbinical story, well-known in Palestine in Jesus' time, and therefore doubtless familiar to Jesus and his audiences, in which a similar situation was described, but with a telling difference. The first part of the story, that is the part about the owner of the vineyard hiring labourers at different times during the day, was the same; but then, according to that story, the workers who came last worked so hard that they did in one hour as much work as the others had done in the whole day, and so they deserved the same wages. The point then is, and a very interesting point it is, that Jesus took the story but changed its ending. And the change he introduced was most significant. The change was precisely what made the parable his, what gave it its depth, and changed if from a mere exhortation to hard work, to a theological consideration on God's dealings with man at the deepest levels of freedom and grace. Jesus' specific teaching is that God does not like to deal with men on the basis of written contracts and specified conditions, does not want to be limited, obliged, tied down, but wants to be trusted, and to be left free to distribute his graces as he pleases. The attempt to tie him down to man's expectations touches his very essence, his majesty and sovereignty. Hence the angry reaction of the owner of the vineyard: "Can't I do what I want with my money? Can't I do what I want with my graces? Are you to be jealous because I am kind? Are you going to protest because I am generous? Are you going to question my decisions and attack my judgement? I tell you that the first will be last, and the last will be first." God upsets our calculations. His accounts invalidate our equations. And we do not quite like that. We do recognize that he is Lord, but we feel uneasy when we see him act as such. We do not like to hear that the first will be last, because we are trying with all our might to be first. We have forgotten that it is only by giving up our claims and going to sit on the last seat, that we can ever be called to occupy the first.

If the Law is a "curse" (Gal 3:13), why was it ever established? Paul has an enlightening answer: to make us conscious of our transgressions (Rm 3:20, 7:7, Gal 3:19). Paradoxically, the Law is necessary to make us realize that we cannot keep it. "Through the Law I died to the Law." (Gal 2:19). That is the process I have outlined above: the precept, the goal, our conviction that we can reach it by ourselves, our full effort, our failure…, and then, as a result, our acknowledging defeat and turning to God. In other

50

words, the Law is the crocodile in the Hindu story: it makes us exert ourselves, give up and surrender to God. Paul sums up masterfully and forcefully: "Scripture shows that all men are locked up under sin (the work of the Law), so that the Promise could be given through faith in Jesus Christ to those who believe." (3:22). The night of the Law gives way to the dawn of the Promise in the light of faith. We tear down our contract, or, in Paul's experience "we nail it to the cross of Christ" (Col 2:14), open our heart and throw ourselves into God's loving arms, sure that what he will give us is much more than what we can ever claim. We let faith take over, and thus we enter into a new and happier and infinitely richer relationship with God. "The Promise was made on the ground of faith, in order that it might be a matter of sheer grace, and that it might be valid for all Abraham's posterity." (Rm 4:16). We, children of Abraham, are also the children of the Promise.

THE POTTER AND THE CLAY

A favourite biblical image: the potter and the clay. The prophets took it and used it repeatedly in their exhortations to a people that loved images, stories and parables. They had watched the village potter at his work, essential for any community and for any home, had bought his vessels and profited by his art. I too have seen the potter at work in the villages of India. He squats in front of a wheel that turns horizontally, with a large hub on which to place the lump of clay, and a heavy rim that imparts stability and speed to the contraption; he then inserts a stick vertically on a hole in the rim, makes the wheel turn with it, gather momentum, reach maximum speed, and suddenly withdraws the stick, slaps the clay on the flat hub and skilfully buries his fingers into the shapeless mass. And then I see (I am thinking of a concrete occasion in a small village in the gentle glow of the setting sun, with children around and the village cattle returning from the fields in a golden cloud of ethereal dust) I see the miracle of creation, shape after shape emerging from the lifeless lump at the merest touch of the artist's hand. It is a cup now, a jar, a tall flower vase, a flat basin, a slim column, a round bowl... The wheel spins round and round, and the game of

53

creation continues as the clay comes alive in the potter's hands. And now suddenly, with a loud laugh and a sweeping gesture, the artisan lifts the entire mass and dumps it unceremoniously on the floor where it becomes again, with a dead thud, an inert lump of slimy clay. I look with surprise at the village potter..., and I think of Isaiah and Jeremiah.

"These are the words which came to Jeremiah from the Lord: Go down at once to the potter's house, and there I will tell you what I have to say. So I went down to the potter's house and found him working at the wheel. Now and then a vessel he was making out of the clay would be spoilt in his hands, and then he would start again and mould it into another vessel to his liking. Then the word of the Lord came to me: Can I not deal with you, Israel, says the Lord, as the potter deals with his clay? You are clay in my hands like the clay in his, O house of Israel." (Jer 18:1-6). "Will the pot contend with the potter, or the earthenware with the hand that shapes it? Will the clay ask the potter what he is making? or his handiwork say to him, 'You have no skill'? Thus says the Lord, Israel's Holy One, his maker: Would you dare question me concerning my children, or instruct me in my handiwork?" (Is 45:9,11). And the Old Testament image carries over into the New, with Paul quoting Isaiah: "Who are you, sir, to answer God back? Can the pot speak to the potter and say, 'Why did you make me like this?'? Surely the potter can do what he likes with the clay. Is he not free to make out of the same lump two vessels, one to be treasured, the other for common use?" (Rm 9:20-21).

If the image of the potter and the clay was a favourite one with the prophets and with Paul, it is definitely not so with us. We feel uneasy before the whims of the potter, and instinctively refuse to see God at the potter's wheel, dealing with his creatures as the potter with the clay. I recognize that the image is dangerous, that it can be misunderstood and be abused, that it can generate fatalism and despair. Historically that is where Calvin got his exaggerated predestination theory and his doctrine of the irrestibleness of divine grace. I was warned as a theology student not to use easily this image from the pulpit, and I see wisdom in that advice. Still, I bring here the potter because I believe that we have gone to the other extreme, and a correction is needed. The voluntarism and selfism and emphasis on freedom and independence and personality and responsibility, the cult of democracy that threatens to invade theology (I once heard a sermon on Christ the King which witty parishioners at once referred to as the sermon on Christ the President), and the humanism that makes man the center of the universe with God only on its far-off edges... are contributing to create an impression, even in spiritual persons, that man is in practice independent of God, and he shapes his own destiny and lives his own life, while God is only a remote witness, a kind well-wisher and the final judge of the ultimate result. That is a false view. The balance between God's sovereign dominion over man, and man's genuine freedom in life is a very delicate one, with the needle inclining now one way now the other, and heresies on both sides across the ages. My stand is that we at present incline towards over-independence from God, and so a look at the other side is healthy and timely, and even necessary. We have buried the potter's wheel, and it is time to dig it up and take a look at it. I personally rejoice to see myself as a small lump of clay in the hands of the divine Potter without any claims, demands or expectations; and I do not feel any fear or misgivings in that situation, because I know he is my Father, and will create in my flesh a better vessel of grace than I could ever manage by myself. I love the potter's wheel.

I need hardly point out that the wheel is the Promise that leaves God full play and initiative, as against the assurances and reservations of the Law, which is the clay that would ask for a clear and binding statement on what was going to happen to it, before it would consent to be placed on the hub of the potter's wheel for treatment. And again, the divine freedom expressed in the outburst, Can't I do what I want with my clay? is an echo of that of the Gospel, Can't I do what I want with my money? It is one continuous teaching from prophets through Gospel to Paul, one current of thought through the Bible, one essential attitude of the Christian before himself and before God. And that is the attitude of faith. The attitude of trust, of confidence, of letting oneself be taken in the hands of God like a lump of clay, without raising questions or asking for guarantees. Our age tends to rationalize everything, to minimize the supernatural, to demythologize, to secularize. No wonder faith is on the decline both as belief and as commitment, as motive power and as living force. Only when God is supreme Lord will faith spring forth in full bloom. We live on a diminished concept of God, and therefore on a stunted faith. We need to come back fully and radically to the basic confession of our faith: Jesus is Lord. The lordship of God does not hamper the freedom of man; on the contrary, it mysteriously and radically establishes it and safeguards it.

Cardinal Danielou finds the same doctrine in another fundamental episode of the Bible, and expresses it with clarity and courage. I quote him, not only for his authority and scholarship, but also because the point to be made is hard and unusual, and I want for myself the protection of a weighty quotation when I am taking the risk of proposing an unpopular doctrine, necessary and wholesome though it is. The occasion for the doctrine is the fact that God in Genesis rejected Cain (the older brother) and accepted Abel (the younger), and the reason for it. The reason, the Cardinal explains, is not, as commonly believed, that Abel (a shepherd) offered good victims for the sacrifice while Cain (a tiller of the soil) offered bad fruits. Nothing of the kind. Cain's fruits and vegetables were as good in their kind as Abel's sucklings in theirs. The Genesis text is perfectly neutral there, though the "later tradition" (Hb 11:4) referred to by the Cardinal took another view. "Abel was a shepherd and Cain a tiller of the soil. The day came when Cain brought some of the produce of the soil as a gift to the Lord; and Abel brought some of the first-born, that is the sucklings, of his flock. The Lord received Abel and his gift with favour; but Cain and his gift he did not receive. Cain was very angry and his face fell." (Gen 4:3-6). Here is the brave quotation behind which I take shelter. "The fact that Yahweh's approval is designed to justify the sacrifice of blood and to affirm its pre-eminence (Cain offered fruits of the earth, while Abel the first-born of his flock), and consequently that such approval owes nothing to the mental dispositions of Abel and Cain, presents us with a paradoxical situation. We have to recognize, in fact, that God accepted Abel's sacrifice and rejected Cain's for no other reason than His own free choice. The wish to minimize that fact, as later tradition did, is to preclude any understanding of the drama that follows and consequently to veil the very mystery which this passage reveals to us at the very beginning of Holy Writ, as the very heart of the cosmic convenant, and one which we meet again and again in Holy Scripture. The mystery in question is that of divine election. Abel is not chosen because he is righteous. He is righteous because he is chosen. God's love is given to him without any previous merit on his part. It is the very mystery of grace in all its paradox. But this mystery, which baffles human reason and so often arouses revolt, is one which forces us to leave our own beaten paths to read the ways of God and make acquaintance with a higher order of things in the world of reality. For if we were going to be judged according to strict justice we should all merit damnation; it is ultimately better for us to rely only on mercy. Abel is the first of those elect, chosen by God on the very threshold of human history, in the heart of a pagan world, to be the first object of the outpourings of Love." (Holy Pagans of the Old Testament, p. 35).

When I myself first read that page I was shocked by it, though from the first I knew it to be true. It is hard, very hard indeed, to say that Abel was not chosen because he was righteous, but was righteous because he was chosen. This can be misinterpreted as blind predestinism that makes of man a lifeless toy in the hands of a whimsical God. The danger is there, and we all recognize it easily and guard ourselves from it instinctively. What we do not so easily realize is that the danger in the opposite direction is just as great, namely the danger of making of man an independent being that lives his life on his own strength and cruises the earth practically on his own steam, with only lip service paid to God's sovereignty and dominion over him. The error that minimizes God's role in man's life is an even greater theological error than the one that minimizes man's role in it, and yet we easily lapse into the greater error and handle our lives as though they in practice depended only on us and our strength and our efforts, with an occasional prayer thrown in, almost more to keep God informed of our progress than to make it truly depend on him. And if we offer sacrifices, we believe, in popular Genesiacal interpretation, that it is they that compel God's approval, rather than God's approval that makes them acceptable, and so of all our "good works": We feel we are accepted by God because we are righteous, not the other way

about. It is precisely because we are wedded to this interpretation of our lives as (practically) independent of God,
that we are shaken when suddenly taken to the other end of
the thesis and made to see them as (practically) subject from
beginning to end to God's ordering of them. The very shock
we receive is proof that we needed the reminder.

The Cardinal knows his ground, and, quietly and
efficiently, makes his point for the uphill belief: we are better
off leaving our lives to God's mercy than trying to run them
on our own. If we want to stand on our own righteousness,
we shall soon find we have nowhere to stand on. In our
terminology again, we shall be wiser to choose the Promise
than the Law. "For all alike have sinned, and are deprived
of God's glory." (Rm 3:23). If we want to plead our justice,
we stand no chance. "If a man keeps the whole law apart
from one single point", warns St. James, "he is guilty of
breaking the whole of it." (Jm 2:10). And his argument, of
course, is unanswerable, as he who violates any precept of
the law disobeys the giver of the law, which is the main
offence. We stand convicted, and we know it. However
appealing to our pride may be the idea of ourselves running
our lives, counting our wages and earning our recompense.
we have reluctantly to accept that we are not going to get
very far that way, and that God's mercy, if we only let him
take over, will take us much farther and higher than our own
scant justice. There is only one more remark I want to make
before leaving Cain and Abel. God chose Abel in preference
to Cain, the younger brother in place of the older, as he did
later when he chose Isaac rather than Ishmael, Jacob rather
than Esau, and David rather than any of his seven older
brothers..., down to the Gospels where the parable of the
prodigal son ends with the younger brother enjoying the
feast in his father's house while his elder brother is still

59

brooding outside. That is a repeated parable in action, a biblical constant that proclaims God's predilection for the humblest and lowest, and emphasizes the point he likes to make of upsetting men's calculations and betraying expectations based on rank, merit, age or tradition. The last will be forever first. The youngest son inherits all, while the obvious heir goes away empty-handed. The smallest lump of clay is taken for the chosen vessel. The last labourer gets full wages. "To shame the wise, God has chosen what the world counts folly, and to shame what is strong, God has chosen what the world counts weakness. He has chosen things low and contemptible, mere nothings, to overthrow the existing order. And so there is no place for human pride in the presence of God." (1 Cor 1:27-29).

God shatters our security. The Bible uses another concept with which we, modern men, are also rather unfamiliar, as with the previous concepts of this chapter, and from which we find ourselves distanced in our understanding of responsibility and guilt. That is the concept of hidden sins. By that are not meant sins hidden from the view or knowledge of others, but hidden from the sinner himself. Sins committed by me, but of which I myself am not aware. It sounds, again, a primitive concept, but it is clear and insistent and unavoidable. That is the prayer of psalm nineteen: "Who is aware of his unwitting sins? Cleanse me of my secret faults." And Paul avows: "I have nothing on my conscience, but that does not mean I stand acquitted." (1 Cor 4:4). Whatever our efforts at innoncence, and at prompt repentance when we fall short of innocence, we cannot be sure that our record is straight. Self-reliance will get us nowhere. The point I want to make is not that of making sure of our eternal salvation in its ultimate expression of going to heaven or to hell, but the more radical one of ensuring such salvation in the making, that is, our spiritual progress, our life in the spirit, our growth in faith, that will eventually flower into glory in the eternal presence of God. That whole process is better looked after when placed in the hands of God than when held tight in our grip as though we were bent on seeing it through at all costs by ourselves. "I do not even pass judgement on myself: my judge is the Lord." (1 Cor 4:3). Everything is in his hands, and that is the best place where it can be.

One more biblical image, or rather a parable in history that illustrates the ways God deals with his people in their pilgrimage, and therefore with us in our lives. When the people of Israel took possession of the Promised Land, the original arrangement was that all the previous inhabitants of those lands would be evicted, so that Israel would be left in full command to live in peace and worship Yahweh in purity of faith. Yet Yahweh himself changed the arrangement later, and permitted some hostile tribes to remain within the boundaries of Israel and harass his people now and again. Four reasons are given in the books of Joshua and Judges for this new disposition on the part of God: it was to be a punishment for their not having kept the Law; a continued test "to see whether or not they will keep strictly to the way of the Lord as their forefathers did" (Jgs 2:22); a training to keep them fit to fight (3:2); and finally a reminder that victory had not come from "their sword or their bow" (Jos 24:12) but from God who fought for them. "These are the nations which the Lord left as a means to test the Israelites: the five lords of the Philistines, all the Canaanites, the Sidonians, and the Hivites who live in Mount Lebanon from Mount Baal-hermon as far as Lebo-hamath" (Jgs 3:3). I am here interested in the last reason given for the coexistence of Hivites and Philistines with Israelites: to remind them that it was not they that had conquered the land by their own strength. Vital reminder. And we all stand in dire need of it. We have an inborn persisting tendency to attribute to ourselves the successes of our spiritual life, the resistance we offer to temptation, the devotion we achieve, the discipline we keep and the good works we do. Surely we thank God for all that, but in our heart of hearts we congratulate ourselves on our exploits, and secretly worship our sword and our bow. We take as done by us what is done by God in us; even obvious graces from heaven stick to the soul and seem after some time to be connatural to us and springing from us. That is spiritual pride of the worst kind, and if it really takes hold of a soul, it is enough to stop any spiritual progress at all. The disease is as dangerous as it is common. And the practical remedy for it is to leave Philistines and Canaanites in our back yard, to leave within us passions and weaknesses and temper and laziness, and let us get now and again a beating at their hands. If the previous victory was ours, why do we now flee? If it was our sword and our bow, where are they now? Every defeat is a reminder, and every fall an eye-opener. The fact that we fall is not important, but the hopeful effect of the fall to make us turn to God and depend on him and recognize that all previous achievements were from him, and from him will have to come all future ones, is such a necessary lesson that it outweighs the fall and soothes its hurt. God be blessed for the Philistines.

ATHENS AND CORINTH

If the first great enemy of faith is Pelagianism (and that has taken three chapters), the second is sophistication (and that deserves at least one chapter). We are just too clever for God, we think too much and analyze too much, we take everything to pieces and want to know how each one works, we study philosophy before theology, and logic before philosophy, and we demand proofs instead of trust, and syllogisms in place of parables. We filter dogma through our brains, and, wonderful though they are, true religious experience is ultimately beyond them; so they suffer trying to grasp it all, feeling in themselves the tension between the obedience of faith and the demands of reason. Man's reason bears herself with queenly deportment, is accustomed to sit on the throne and to have her dictates accepted as supreme ruling among thinking men. She will not surrender her sceptre without a struggle, and in the struggle she causes confusion, misunderstanding and pain. True, when faith joins hands with reason, their union bears the happiest fruits of spiritual understanding and heavenly wisdom; but the way to that union is paved with difficulties.

This is an incident that amused me. Once I, together with some Jesuit companions, attended a ten-day meditation course given by a world-known Buddhist teacher who initiated us with great zeal, competence and earnestness in the exacting and systematic art of traditional Buddhist spirituality as expressed in one of its most ancient ways of meditation. Most of the day, from four o'clock in the morning, was taken up by long "sittings" in heroic immobility under his guidance and in his presence in the large, austere meditation hall; but he also gave us detailed instructions and theoretical inputs on the principles behind the practice he taught so well and exemplified in his person. And during those talks I could not help smiling secretly to myself (which was all that the stern discipline and absolute silence of those purposeful days would allow) as I began to notice clearly and amusingly the pains he took to appease and conciliate the Jesuits in his audience. There were many others in the course, people of different ages, occupations, religions, there were Hindus, Jains and Christians, young people and older men, women and a few nuns among them, but he turned again and again to the few Jesuits in the hall to repeat to us the pointed warning that we were not to discuss, to question, to debate in our minds (let alone with others!) the ideas and methods offered to us on those days, because of the real danger of ruining the exercises of ten days with the ideas of a lifetime. After the course we were free, he said, to criticize and refute and reject all that we wanted, but not during the experience. He requested us to set our thoughts aside, not to judge or condemn, not even to accept or evaluate, but simply to trust him and do as he said for ten days. He sought us with his eyes in the hall, addressed us, reminded us, and not a day passed without his singling us out for the expected warning. I said that I smiled when the warning came, and I smiled because I knew the background.

64

The good old master had had previous experience of Jesuits—and had grown wary of them. Two Jesuits, of a rather intellectual bent of mind, had taken part in a similar experience with him some time before. Now, each day he had allowed questions, both in public at the end of the daily talk, and in private during personal interviews, and those two Jesuits had taken full advantage of every such opportunity to show their training. They had plagued him with questions, doubts, arguments, they had tried to engage him in discussion, to argue with him, to score over him, they had called into question every statement and every directive, and had only succeeded in tiring him and changing a meditation experience into a theological duel. He wanted to forestall such a situation with us, and warned us in time. He did not know that we too had already been warned at our end! We knew of the exploits of our two predecessors, and we asked no questions. There are times when the mind, however highly trained, is best told to stand aside and keep quiet for a while. Thought can hamper experience.

I myself have been some times the victim of such over-intellectualism in religious people. I have often directed spiritual retreats and meditation camps for priests and religious, and I know the formidable resistance some intellectual types can offer to guidance and prayer and faith. Once, directing a thirty-day retreat for men, I encountered a young priest who, in his regular daily visits to me for direction, made it a point, instead of speaking about himself as he should have done, to let me know without fail that in my talks to the group that day I had contradicted myself with respect to something I had said the previous day. He had a real knack for finding contradictions in all I said, and he triumphantly showed them to me day after day. Patience is not my strong point, though while conducting a retreat I have of necessity to make a show of it for good effect, but in that case even the show came to an end, and one day I confronted my spirited opponent: "Listen," I said, "I am not such a fool as to contradict myself at such short notice. A contradiction is a big thing, and I could not manage one per day even if I honestly tried. But be that as it may, what I want to tell you is what you are doing with this game of contradiction-hunting you are so vigorously indulging in. You don't want to get into the retreat, you don't want to observe silence, you don't want to pray; you are afraid to face God and to face yourself, and in order to avoid what could prove a rather unpleasant experience for you, you divert your energies to the futile pastime of finding contradictions in my talks. You are exercising your brains instead of your heart, and occupying yourself with my talks instead of with your prayers. Keep it up, and you'll manage to get through the thirty days unscathed. I don't want to play judge and condemn you, but I do know and I want you to know that there is no better defence mechanism against God's action in the soul in days of grace than the smoke screen of intellectual activity let loose in the middle of what should be a devotional experience. If you are really interested in your soul's welfare I heartily recommend you to stop looking for contradictions in my talks, or, still better, to stop coming to my talks altogether. You will surely make a better retreat." I fully appreciate the work of the intellect, but I also know its limitations and its mischief. It can ruin a man's prayer; and prayer is the food of faith.

In such prayer experiences I have found priests who tell me they cannot meditate on the scenes of Jesus' infancy because they consider them unhistorical, or on the apparitions of the risen Christ, which for them are mythical; or who, again, are distracted by any Gospel reference, since

66

the first thing it suggests to them is not its obvious salvific meaning, but its level of authenticity at the hands of scholars in the latest research. Research again is wonderful, but when it interferes with devotion it can do harm. I am in no way opposing studies or blaming scholars, but pointing out a danger we all have in our life of faith. An exemplary priest, who was professor of Holy Scripture, told me once that he found it impossible to pray the psalms with devotion any more, much though he loved them. He had studied them, taught them, written on them, and now when he took them up for his daily liturgical prayer, his mind was at once filled with interpretations, quotations, cross-references, alternative readings, doubtful renderings, questions he had been asked about them and answers he had given. And that was the end of his prayer. For him the psalms had ceased to be a source of devotion, and had become matter for the classroom, they were not inspired prayers for him any more, but a syllabus for an examination. He knew too much to enjoy them any more. This, of course, need not always be so, and not all Scripture professors are estranged from the psalms. Scholarship can coexist with devotion, and learning with simplicity. In fact, when knowledge of the sacred sciences is combined with transparency of faith and spontaneity in prayer, we get the beautiful result of a learned saint and a devout scholar. Their race, however, is not numerous.

We hear of divine communications to men and women in different countries and times and circumstances. Usually the recipients of such heavenly favours are simple shepherds or young peasant girls; we do not hear of such communications being granted to leading theologians or ecclesiastical officials, worthy though they are in every respect. One of the questions Bernardette had to answer in cross-examination was why, if Our Lady wanted a chapel to be erected there, she had not revealed that directly to the bishop, instead of doing it though her. She modestly represented that it was not for her to answer that question. We are left to wonder what shape Our Lady's dialogues would have taken if they had taken place with a trained theologian instead of a simple country girl. Our Lady surely must have felt more at home with a girl who almost reminded her of herself in her spontaneous simplicity and easy candour. I can sympathise with the heartfelt cry of St. Augustine in the midst of his wisdom and knowledge: "The illiterates are rising up, and are taking the Kingdom of Heaven from our hands!" The saintly doctor of the Church almost seemed to wish he were illiterate. For some things it can be an advantage.

Another great theologian, Karl Barth, felt also the dead weight of sophistication in the lives of serious students of theology, and used his own scholarship and his sense of humour to describe from the other end, that is from God's end, the dampening effect of too much intellectualism on the relationship between God and man. The prophet Amos, in a celebrated passage, had expressed in strong language God's condemnation of the rites and sacrifices which his people offered him without putting their heart into them: "I hate, I spurn your pilgrim feasts; I will not delight in your sacred ceremonies. When you present your sacrifices and offerings I will not accept them, nor look on the buffaloes of your sacred-offerings. Spare me the sound of your songs; I cannot endure the music of your lutes..." (Am 5:21-23). The theologian now parodies the text, putting theological volumes in place of buffaloes, and the dissertations of dogmatic treatises in place of the music of lutes: "I hate, I despise your lectures and seminars, your sermons, papers and bible commentaries, and I will not smell your discussions, conferences and vacation courses. Though you offer one another and me your hermeneutical, dogmatic, ethical and pastoral recommendations, I will not accept them; neither will I regard the peace offerings of your fat beasts. Take away from me the noise of the old theologians' massive tomes and that of the young theologians' dissertations. And I will not hear the melody of the reviews that you publish in your theological journals, letters and surveys, and in your church and literary papers." Apparently God does not feel happy either when the formalism of concepts replaces the warmth of devotion in his people, when the mind silences the heart, and discourse weakens faith. God does not feed on syllogisms.

Many priests have told me their mothers pray better than they do. I, smilingly, give them one reason: their mothers have not had three years of philosophy, four of theology and one of pastoral reflection, as they have had. This, again, is not disparaging sacred studies, which I value and defend and have myself enjoyed in full measure, but to point out a definite shortcoming they have, a defect which, at times, may defeat the very purpose of such serious studies and long training. They sharpen criticism, which is an essential tool of research, but which is also a disturbing intruder into the sacred intimate dealings of God with the soul. It is like bringing a detective into a courtship, or a psychoanalyst into the marriage chamber. Likely to cast a pall on the proceedings. Without going to extremes, as Zen does when it calls thought "the disease of the human mind", or Luther did when he spoke of reason as "the devil's bride", we recognize that unbridled thought and desultory reason can play havoc if let loose in the delicate chambers where God and the soul meet in secret company. The "Poor Little Dove", as St. Theresa familiarly called the Holy Spirit, may not feel inclined to flutter around if the air is thick with hawks and kites.

69

"Unless you become like little children, you will not enter the Kingdom of Heaven." "I thank you, Father, Lord of heaven and earth, because you have hidden these things from the learned and wise, and have revealed them to little children." "What, you are a teacher in Israel and you don't know these things?" "I will destroy the wisdom of the wise, and annihilate the cleverness of the clever." The original climate in which the Gospel was born was one of simplicity and candour, and it is the same climate that will make it grow and prosper and flower in our hearts. We have to become like little children. Little children enjoy the unspoilt intuition to know when and on whom they can place their trust, even if they do not conceptualize their mental processes or categorize their thinking; and they relax charmingly when they sense they are loved and protected. They do not ask for guarantees, they just smile and lose themselves in their games when they realize they are among friendly people. And God is always friendly, if only we have not lost the innate sense to recognize it in our hearts, before our minds start asking questions. A true child knows his father.

Here is another biblical parable in action, meant for us to discover its meaning and assimilate its teaching. Jesus continues to teach in parables after his death, inviting to listen those who would listen, and to understand those who would understand. The story is in the book of Acts, and I tell it in parable fashion. There was an ardent follower of Jesus, named Paul, who wanted to bring the name of his Lord and Master to the whole world, and with that ideal in his heart directed his steps to the intellectual capital of the world he knew, Athens, and sought by all possible means to establish among its citizens the faith in the Lord Jesus. He took pains as he never had taken in any city so far, he planned his campaign and implemented it step by step. He contacted the intellectuals in the city and arranged meetings with representatives of the two main schools of thought at the time among them, the Epicureans and the Stoics, till he succeeded in getting himself invited for a talk in the most exclusive circle of intellectual life in Athens, the Court of Areopagus. He prepared his speech as he had never prepared any speech in his life, thought up an elaborate opening paragraph as the rules of rhetoric taught in his day, seeking to hold the attention of his listeners from the start by alluding to the altar "To the Unknown God" he had seen in Athens, proof of the accommodating religious spirit of the Greek people, and from which Paul took the lead, rather artificially though not without effect, to speak to them about "the God whom you worship without knowing him"; then he took care to select and memorize quotations from some well-known Greet poets, Epimenides of Knosos, Aratus of Cilicia and Cleantus the Stoic, a gesture calculated to win acceptance and facilitate the essential message, and finally he eloquently plunged into the need for repentance before the man who had been sent to judge the world, as he had been raised from the dead for that mission. A fine speech it was—yet it went flat. Some openly scoffed at the newcomer, others, with more Athenian tact, let him out gently with the politely disguised dismissal, "We'll listen to you some other time". There was even a joke making the rounds of the agora those days, that a stranger had come to preach about Jesus and his resurrection, while people had understood him to proclaim a new divine couple, Jesus and Anastasia, mistaking the Greek word for "resurrection" (anastasis), which the Jew from Tarsus possibly mispronounced, for a proper name which they made into the name of a goddess (Anastasia). Demosthenes, who knew well his fellow citizens, had said in his most famous speech that the main business of the Athenians was to idle

71

about in the forum asking each other, "What is the latest news?"; and Luke, who may possibly have read the stricture in Demosthenes' *"Peri tou Stephanou"*, perhaps the world's greatest oration, echoed its criticism in sharp parallel words: "The Athenians have no time for anything but talking or hearing the latest novelty." (Ac 17:21). Full-time professionals of pseudo-intellectual gossip. Barren ground for the seed of the Gospel.

Paul left Athens with a depressing sense of utter failure. Athens had closed its doors to the Gospel. There would be no church established there, no new visit, no apostolic letter ever addressed to the city that was the intellectual centre of the world. Paul proceeded to his next destination, near-by Corinth, still in Greece, and he fell into a despondent mood. There was the fatigue of the last few days, the effort, the failure, the realization that he was up against a wall and progress would be impossible for the Gospel in the Greek world—which was the best of cultures. Paul almost gave up. Athens had been enough! And now Corinth. Fine place for the Gospel! Corinth was Europe's first great harbour on the way from Asia Minor, and collected to itself all the filth that came from the East and from the West. The very name "Corinth" was synonymous with vice, "to live like a Corinthian" meant to lead a dissolute life, and "a Corinthian girl" was a prostitute. The Acrocorinth was a meeting place for their trade, and sailors of the seven seas knew it. If Athens was the capital of Greek thought, Corinth was the capital of its vice. This historical situation is sharply reflected in Paul's own subsequent letters to the city, long passages of which deal with current sexual excesses in Corinth, in condemnation of "unclean lives, fornication and sensuality" No wonder he was in low spirits, and Corinth, after Athens, had depressed him beyond endurance. To make matters

72

worse, when he got some companions to join him and started preaching again, he met again opposition and feared for the future. And then God intervened. The Lord visited him at night, as he did at times of crisis in the life of his chosen apostle, and comforted him with his presence, his word and a startling and encouraging revelation: "Don't be afraid...; I am with you...; I have many people in this city." (Ac 18:10). Jesus knew well that the greatest comfort for Paul was to know that in that city "he had many people", that many would listen to his message and accept the Gospel and form another young church. That hope would give new life to Paul, as in fact it did. Paul, who had withdrawn to a private house, took up his task again with enthusiasm, stayed in Corinth for the record time of a year and a half at a stretch, and when he finally moved on he left there a flourishing church to which the largest volume of extant Pauline correspondence was addressed.

And the meaning of the parable? That sensual Corinth proved a better ground for the Gospel than proud Athens, that lust is a smaller obstacle to grace than pride, that the seed, that was smothered by the supercilious Athenians, grew readily among simple Corinthians, tainted though they were with sexual disorders. A sophisticated mind shuts off divine action more effectively than an impure body. Human weaknesses do not hinder God's work in the soul, while human pride does. Corinth harbours a growing church, while Athens remains barren. There is no "Church of Athens" in New Testament writings as there is a "Church of Corinth" and a "Church of Philippi". In licentious Corinth Jesus has many people; in intellectual Athens he has next to none. Corinth is remembered by grateful Christians today as the church of the charisms, of the song of love (1 Cor 13), of the outpouring of the Spirit. Athens, in Christian memory,

73

remains as the unhappy record of an initial failure. Stoics and Epicureans continue to debate idly in the agora the latest "word-sower", and the city, that was the brains of the world, decays into forgotten irrelevance. Let him, who has ears to hear with, hear.

The parable is not isolated. I have quoted before chapter eleven of the epistle to the Hebrews, and shall quote it again later as an essential treatise of faith in the New Testament. The chapter lists a few chosen names, outstanding links in the chain of faith that binds together the different chapters in time of the history of the people of God. In the list there is an unlikely, almost embarrassing name: Rahab. The prostitute of Jericho is mentioned as a carrier of faith in the privileged roster, her profession being no obstacle to the prophetic meaning of her action in helping Israel's spies. She is listed in between Moses and Abraham and David. Yet the name of king Solomon, wisest of the wise, does not appear in the list of Israel's milestones in the faith. Athens is forgotten once more, while Corinth wins again.

What side am I on? Athens or Corinth? By sin I am a Corinthian. Let me be a Corinthian too in simplicity and humility to escape the ruins of Athens.

FAITH THROUGH PRAYER

I was once talking of religious matters with a Hindu
thinker whose works I admire, when he said to me: "I do
have some faith..., and I wish I had more." I reflected with
him that we all are in that position, and that it is explicitly
recorded in the Gospels, when the father of an epileptic
boy, who sought his cure, spoke thus before Jesus: "I have
faith; help me where faith falls short." Jesus accepted the
prayer, and healed the boy. Faith is the beginning of the
Gospel: "Repent and believe the Good News" (Mk 1:15),
and the end of it: "This has been written so that you may
believe" (Jn 20:31). Jesus rejoiced when he found faith, as
in the foreign woman, the "Syrophaenician pagan" who
could not take No for an answer to her plea for her sick
daughter, in the Roman centurion who with charming
military language declared that just as he could order about
his own soldiers so could Jesus command life and death,
and they would obey him, and in Peter at Caesarea Philippi
when he spoke beyond flesh and blood what only the Father
could have revealed him. And then Jesus suffered, was
grieved, frustrated when he met unbelief, mistrust, lack of
faith. He could not help people in their needs in his own

home town of Nazareth where he was "taken aback" by their unbelief. he complained bitterly of lack of faith in "this wicked generation", he wondered aloud with wounded feeling. "How long will I have to put up with you?" He even mused in front of his disciples, in what was perhaps the most despondent statement that ever came from his lips, "Will the Son of Man find any faith on earth when he comes again?" He called his apostles "men of little faith", and even after his Resurrection he rebuked them for their lack of faith. (Mk 16:14).

Jesus' insistence on faith was not entirely lost on his disciples; they had marked his behaviour, his utter trust in the Father who always heard him, his assurance when commanding nature's forces or man's diseases, his joy at finding faith in others and his anger when missing it, and they did something they seldom managed to do in their dealings with their Master: they got together, spoke among themselves, approached him and put before him a concrete request: "Lord, increase our faith." That was a beautiful prayer which sums up our own aspiration: increase, because we have some already; and increase, because we want more. Jesus' answer was to open their eyes to what they could do if they had real faith, with the picturesque example of telling a tree to uproot itself and be planted in the sea, and, beneath the example, to direct their attention to the channel of faith that brings down the power and grace of heaven to act among men, that is petitionary prayer. It is by asking the Father that trees can be uprooted—and vices too. Pray in faith, and you will obtain all that you need. Faith is the greatest power on earth, and prayer its exercise. Petitionary prayer increases faith, directly, by asking for it, and, indirectly, by asking for other things with faith in Jesus' promises and seeing that faith confirmed when the petition is granted. Ask and you will receive. Grow in faith by practicing prayer; and practice prayer by asking God for what you need, in virtue of his love and his promise. A father gives his children what they need and ask for, and so to ask God for favours is to assert our faith in him as Father. Prayer is faith in action. Ask, and your faith will grow.

This looks easy, but I warn you it is not. Prayer of petition is the first prayer we learn, and even a child understands it; yet it grows harder as the child becomes a young man and the young man an adult. It is not easy to ask, because it is not easy to believe that we are going to get what we are asking. It is not easy to ask, because petition is submission, is dependence, is humility and is commitment. Petition can be routine, of course, and then it means nothing, but when it is serious, it engages the whole man before God, before himself and before others, it sums up religion and embodies faith, it defines man and tempers his life. That is why, when taken seriously, petitionary prayer elicits sharp opposite reactions from different kinds of people. I have before my eyes a few telling testimonies: a Vedantin says that prayer of petition is "below man's dignity"; a Marxist calls it "a slave's appeal"; for a Zenist it is "idle entertainment"; while a Freudian sees in it "the projection of an indigent mind". On the other side, for a devout enlightened Christian it is "the summary of all that is best in religious man: in it there is adoration, humility, trust that is love, and faith that is commitment; there is thanks-giving and joy in the reception of gifts, and there is acceptance of God's will in leaving the outcome to him".

In fact, when Jesus was asked by his disciples to teach them how to pray, he taught them petitionary prayer: "Give us bread...; your Kingdom come." And yet, if one could speak of fashions in spirituality (and, with due respect, there *are* such fashions), today among large sections of prayerful Christians the tendency is towards contemplative practices, Eastern types of meditation, Zen techniques, awareness exercises, which are wonderful in themselves, but may at times relegate to oblivion the fundamental practice of petitionary prayer. This would be a great loss. The basic Christian attitude is the longing for the Kingdom, and every prayer of petition, from the daily bread to the fulfillment of God's will, is, in its own little, humble, fragmented way, a part and an echo of the one great all-embracing petition: Your Kingdom come. That final desire is actualized in the thousand concrete situations of our daily life, and every time we lift our eyes to God and make a request, however small, we are standing on faith and are asking for the Kingdom. May the Kingdom come today in token and in sign, so that it may come one day in its fullness. To pray is to anticipate the parousia.

The petitionary prayer that kindles faith in the soul is the earnest, determined, purposeful one, not the routine repetition of set formulae, or the soulless expression of standard wants. That is the danger of our petitions. If somebody is sick we are supposed to pray for his recovery, if there is a drought we pray for rain, and if there is war somewhere in the world, we pray for peace. Such prayers are fine, but the trouble with them is that our heart is not quite in them. We make those prayers because they are the right thing to do, we express the proper request with the proper words at the proper time—and we stop there. That is the rubric, the custom, the ceremony. The right grace prayed for—without expecting to receive it. The blessing requested—without real hope to obtain it. "The great temptation in prayer is to become conventional, to pray in pious language for the things for which we know we ought to pray. But the truth is that at least sometimes no one would be more shocked than we would be, if our prayer was granted. We may pray for the giving up of some habit — without the slightest intention of giving it up. We may pray for some virtue or quality — without any real desire to possess it. We may pray to be made into a certain kind of person — when the last thing that we in fact want is to be changed, and when we are very well content to be as we are. The peril of prayer is pious and unmeaning platitudes. The danger of prayer is that we very correctly ask for 'the right things', with no desire to receive them." (Barclay). We pray dutifully for the things we should pray for, but we do not rule our lives by our prayer.

John the Baptist's father, Zechariah, had been praying all his life, as a good Jew and a good priest, for the coming of the Messiah. That was the official prayer, the regular petition, the central expectation embedded in the conscience of the people of God and expressed in its daily prayers. That was the very essence of the Temple liturgy and of the service every Sabbath at the synagogue. "Send down your dew, Oh heavens, and let the clouds rain down the Just One; let the earth open up and bring forth the Saviour." Zechariah knew the message well, led the people in prayer for its fulfillment, and himself prayed for it, especially that week when he had been appointed for duty in the sanctuary. He had prayed for the coming of the Messiah, and yet when the angel appeared to him and spoke in terms which to anyone versed in the prophets were open messianic language announcing· the proximity of the Expected One, he did not believe him, and was made dumb for a period for his unbelief. Too good to be true, he must have thought. I did pray for that, but, really, I never quite expected it to happen; not in my lifetime anyhow, and not in any connection with my family. Do we not, priests and religious, fall at times in the same routine of praying in beautiful words for the things we know we are supposed to pray for, without seriously expecting them to happen? We could possibly profit by being struck dumb for a while at the hands of a visiting angel.

Peter had been put in prison by king Herod, and all his friends in Jerusalem were praying for him, afraid as they were that he could meet the same fate as James, who had been beheaded just then in the same prison to please the people. Peter found himself freed by an angel, and as soon as he checked his bearings he made for a house where he would feel safe, the house of John Mark, Paul's helper for a time and later Peter's helper too, possibly the author of the second gospel. A prayer meeting was going on precisely then at the house, with the burning intention of Peter's safety as the center of the prayer. Peter knocked. A maid, Rhoda, went to the door. She shouted the news in joy: "Peter is here!" And she got a cold response from the group: "You must be crazy." Nobody believed her. That is, those good Christians did not believe their own prayer. They were praying for Peter's deliverance. Peter is delivered, and their reaction is: Impossible! It is comforting to realize that God hears imperfect prayers. And it is disturbing to think that even devout people can pray without actually meaning what they say.

When Tobias asked Sarah's father, Raguel, to give him his daughter in marriage, Raguel was worried and feared that Tobias would die the first night as seven other bridegrooms had done before him. On the other hand he could not refuse because of family ties, and so he gave his permission together with a prayer and a blessing that nothing untoward should happen to the brave young man. Yet, practical man that he was, he ordered his servants to dig a grave quietly at night and have it ready in the morning—just in case. Only when he verified early next day that Tobias had survived the family curse, did he give orders to fill in the grave at once before full daylight, so that his neighbours would not learn of the precaution he had taken—practical man that he was. He gave the blessing and he dug the grave. He did not have much faith in his own blessing.

Now a Hindu story. The guru's ashram was by the side of a large river, and so it was with astonishment that he heard from his disciples how the shepherd girl who brought milk daily from the other side of the river, did so walking dry-shod over the deep running waters. He called the girl, and asked her whether that was so. She said, "Of course". The guru inquired further, "Do you think I can do the same?" She again said, "Of course; you have only to go on repeating aloud the name of God as I do, and you will cross safely on the waters." The guru decided to give it a try. They walked, the girl in front, and the guru behind. He stepped gingerly ahead, faithfully repeating the name of God; but then, afraid that his saffron tunic would get wet in the water, he lifted it carefully with his hand as his feet trod the waters. And, of course, he kept sinking lower and lower as he advanced. The girl looked back, saw his plight, and exclaimed with innocent laughter, "Not that way, my master, not that way! The name of the Lord on your lips and the edge of your tunic in your hand…, that is not the way to cross the river!" And she merrily went ahead as the guru turned back crestfallen. Halfhearted prayer is no prayer. Prayer is faith, and faith is commitment, and commitment is of the whole man if it is anything at all. If you have courage, let go of your tunic and walk through life on the strength of God's name: and if not, stay on your side of the river and follow the routine you have always followed. Incidentally, it is again the simple shepherd girl who teaches the learned guru a lesson in faith. The warning against sophistication seems to be universal.

Prayer, when made with sincerity, brings us face to face with God, and makes us deal with him as person to person, with a realism that is the expression and exercise of faith itself. Moses was faced with the impossible task of leading a complex and recalcitrant group of people across inhospitable land against multiple enemies, and his only ally was Yahweh, who had entrusted him with that mission, and whom he approached with a frankness, a familiarity and, at times, a vehemence, which were unheard-of and almost unthinkable for his contemporaries. At Sinai the Lord was angry with his people who had betrayed him to worship the golden calf, and had a rather radical solution in mind, which he proposed to Moses. "So the Lord said to Moses, 'I have considered this people, and I see that they are a stubborn people. Now, let me alone to vent my anger upon them, so that I may put an end to them and make a great nation spring from you.' " (Ex 32:9-10). Moses reacted rather sharply and argued cleverly. He reminded Yahweh of his promise to Abraham, Isaac and Jacob, and, more cunningly, played on what he knew was a sensitive point with Yahweh: the glory of his name, threatened in this case by what the Egyptians would think about him if he carried out his intentions. "But Moses set himself to placate the Lord his God. 'O Lord', he said, 'why should you vent your anger upon your people, whom you brought out of Egypt with great power and a strong hand? Why let the Egyptians say, "So he meant evil when he took them out, to kill them in the mountains and wipe them off the face of the earth"? Turn from your anger, and think better of the evil you intend against your people.' " (11-12). He got what he wanted: "The Lord relented and spared his people the evil with which he had threatened them." (14). Yet the desert journey was long, the hardships many, and the food monotonous; and once again Moses' people became restless under his leadership. "The Israelites wept once again and cried, 'Will no one give us meat? Think of it! In Egypt we had fish for the asking, cucumbers and water-melons, leeks and onions and garlic. Now our throats are parched; there is nothing wherever we look except this manna.' Moses heard the people wailing, all of them by their families at the opening of their tents. Then the Lord became very angry, and Moses was troubled. He said to the Lord, 'Why have you brought trouble on your servant? How have I displeased the Lord that I am burdened with the care of this whole people? Am I their mother? Have I brought them into the world, and am I called upon to carry them in my bosom, like a nurse with her babies, to the land promised by you on oath to their fathers? Where am I to find meat to give them all? They pester me with their wailing and their "Give us meat to eat." This whole people is a burden too heavy for me; I cannot carry it alone. If that is your purpose for me, then kill me outright. But if I have won your favour, let me suffer this trouble at your hands no longer.' " (Nm 11:4-15). Moses had effectively tendered his resignation—knowing very well that it would not be accepted. He knew how to bring pressure on Yahweh, how to bargain, how to get from him even the most unlikely result, like meat in the desert. And he won his point. The wind from the West blew steadily, and quails fell from heaven all around into eager hands. God did punish the people, to keep face somehow after yielding in the main issue, but Moses got fundamentally what he wanted, and Israel marched on.

Yet the main test still lay ahead. Israel had already reached the borders of the Promised Land, and only one last assault separated the wandering people from their final rest. Moses, as usual procedure, sent spies to reconnoitre the land and gather information to plan the last strategy. As the occasion was particularly solemn, he chose one man from each tribe, to have the people fully represented from the beginning of what he thought would be the last campaign. The twelve men departed, took forty days to explore the land, and came back with a bunch of grapes so heavy that it had to be carried on a pole between two men, all taking turns on the job, and with a detailed report of all they had seen and observed. The fruits of the land were outsize, as the specimens they had brought showed abundantly, but then so also were the inhabitants of the land, so large and tall that in their presence "we felt no bigger than grass-hoppers, and that is how we looked to them." The explorers were frightened, felt sure that any attempt to fight those giants was doomed to absolute failure and bitter rout, and they strongly discouraged the people and the leaders from proceeding any farther. That was a sad day in the history of Israel. After crossing the desert, when the end seemed close at hand, they were stopped by the utter impossibility of taking the final step. "Then the whole Israelite community cried out in dismay; all night long they wept. One and all they made complaints against Moses and Aaron: 'If only we had died in Egypt or in the wilderness!' they said. 'Far happier if we had! Why should the Lord bring us to this land, to die in battle and leave our wives and our dependants to become the spoils of war? To go back to Egypt would be better than this.' And they began to talk of choosing someone to lead them back." (Nm 14:1-4). Two of the explorers, Joshua son of Nun, and Caleb son of Jephunneh, had a dissenting opinion from the other ten, and tried to convince the people that the situation was not so grim, and victory was still possible. They had misjudged the mood of the people, who, tired of the weary journey and frustrated at its disappointing end, took stones in their hands, and got ready to apply the ready punishment to the two optimists who wanted them to go ahead. Only Yahweh's timely intervention saved Joshua and Caleb. He appeared in the Tent of the Presence, and the people withdrew, leaving Moses to deal with him. "Then the Lord said to Moses, 'How much longer will this people treat me with contempt? How much longer will they refuse to trust me in spite of all the signs I have shown among them? I will strike them with pestilence. I will deny them their heritage, and you and your descendants I will make into a nation greater and more numerous than they.' But Moses answered the Lord, 'What if the Egyptians hear of it? It was you who brought this people out of Egypt by your strength. What if they tell the inhabitants of this land? They too have heard of you, Lord, that you are with this people, and are seen face to face, that your cloud stays over them, and you go before them in a pillar of cloud by day and in a pillar of fire by night. If then you put them all to death at one blow, the nations who have heard these tales about you will say, "The Lord could not bring this people into the land which he promised them by oath; and so he destroyed them in the wilderness." Now let the Lord's might be shown in its greatness, true to your proclamation of yourself: "The Lord, long-suffering, ever constant, who forgives iniquity and rebellion, and punishes sons to the third and fourth generation for the iniquity of their fathers, though he does not sweep them clean away." You have borne with this people from Egypt all the way here; forgive their iniquity, I beseech you, as befits your great and constant love.' The Lord said, 'Your prayer is answered; I pardon them.' " (11-20). Moses goes back to the argument he knew could not fail. "What if the Egyptians know of it?" They were far away now, but news travel even across the desert, and sooner or later they would learn about it, and would speak ill of Yahweh. And again Yahweh yields to Moses. He will punish the rebels, to be sure, one year for each day of their exploration, that is forty years of wanderings in the desert for the forty days they took to examine the land with such adverse results. But eventually Israel will reach, and Moses will see the land. His prayer had won.

Chapter eleven of the letter to the Hebrews sums up effectively Moses' attitude to God, describing it as that of one "who saw the invisible God as visible". (11.27). That is the reality of faith which Moses experienced and transformed into prayer, guidance and strength. He could dialogue with God, argue with him, force him, almost blackmail him, because for him God was a person, a master, a friend with whom he dealt "face to face". For Moses, prayer was a conversation; the presence of God, visible contact; and faith, reality. If Abraham is our father in the faith, Moses is our example in its practice.

ASK AND YOU WILL RECEIVE

"It may be true that Christianity would be, intellectually, a far easier religion, if it told us to scrap the whole idea of petitionary prayer." That is the responsible opinion, proferred not without personal pain and intimate feeling, of an original theologian and sincere Christian, C.S. Lewis, who himself had prayed with his whole heart, and had seen with unavoidable finality that some times his prayers were not, in any meaningful way, answered. I see more faith in addressing oneself to the question than in glossing it over with superficial piety. Job, who asked questions, pleased God better than his friends, who told him to keep quiet. To grow in faith we must be able to pose questions.

Few points are more stressed in the Gospel than the unconditional promise God gives to answer the petitions made to him. "Ask and you will receive", "whatever you pray for in faith you will receive", "whatever you ask for in prayer, believe that you have received it, and it will.be yours", "if two of you agree on earth about any request you have to make, that request will be granted by my heavenly Father", "if you ask the Father for anything in my name, he will give it to you", "so far you have asked nothing in my name; ask and you will receive, that your joy may be complete ." Joy indeed follows the answered prayer, not only because something has been obtained through it, but also because the procedure has worked, the promise has been kept, because we have been taken into account, and a timely petition has made a difference in our lives. Heaven has listened to earth, and how could the earth but rejoice?

But then, heaven does not always listen. The solemn, clear, repeated promise is not always fulfilled. Prayers are left without answer, and petitions to heaven do not bring down the favours they had confidently requested. "Every war, every famine or plague, almost every death-bed is the monument to a petition that was not granted. It is easy to see why so much more is written about worship and contemplation than about 'crudely' or 'naively' petitionary prayer. The real problem is not why refusal is so frequent, but why the opposite result is so lavishly promised. The New Testament contains embarrassing promises that what we pray for with faith we shall receive. How is this to be reconciled with the observed facts?" (C.S. Lewis). It takes honesty to speak like that. It takes faith to question faith, and the humble inquiry itself deepens the believer's commitment.

When I was a young priest I preached a sermon on this theme, which I had carefully prepared, and in which I said the following: "When you have asked the Lord for some grace, and he has refused to grant it, rejoice! And I will tell you why. When God refuses to give you what you have asked, that means he is granting you two graces instead of one. The first is not granting something which, though you don't realize it, would have been harmful to you; and the second is to grant you later, in his generosity that will never fail, some other bigger grace through your prayer. Thus, you must be doubly grateful when what you ask is not given you. Tell the Lord so, and thank him for not having heard your original prayer. You understand now why." Pretty clever of me, I must say. I even remember someone in the congregation coming up to me after the service and congratulating me on the convincing explanation I had given of why God did not seem to answer our prayers. I felt quite good about it at the time. Today I feel silly. A bit of empty brainwork to cover up the trying reality of man feeling let down by God, and of God remaining free in the very fulfillment of his own promises. Such answers are definitely well-meant, and they can help some people in some circumstances; but in themselves such humanly thought-out answers are only cheap escapes and superficial devices to hide for a moment the unavoidable depth of a permanent mystery. It will be helpful here to revise those answers, to acknowledge their partial help, and to feel, through their very insufficiency, the need to probe deeper in faith.

I read a practical explanation in a book on prayer. It was something like this. On the table where I work there is a lamp that gives me light while I write. Sometimes I switch it on, and yet the light does not light up. When such a thing happens I do not lose faith in physics or curse electricity, but I just think that there is something wrong with my lamp. And in fact there is. The plug is loose or the wire is broken or the bulb is fused. Something in my lamp has to be mended. Something in my prayer has to be corrected. Physics is not to be blamed for my darkness, nor God for my disappointments. Let me check the wiring and fix the connections. Beautiful and candid attitude. And true, no doubt. But only partially. It is a noble thing to take the blame on ourselves, but God's promises, serious and unmistakeable in this case, go far beyond our personal shortcomings into unconditional guarantee. He does not need a perfect lamp.

89

St. Augustine summed up, with one of his favourite plays on words, the reasons for our prayers not being heard: *"mala, male, mali."* We pray for the wrong thing, or in the wrong way, or with the wrong disposition (that is, we are the wrong kind of person). Three "wrongs" that combine to invalidate our petitions and cancel our hopes. Three explanations that cover all our disappointments in prayer. We pray for the wrong thing. We all have said (to ourselves or to others—usually to others) that if a child asks for a knife, his father will do well not to give it to him, lest he hurt himself with it. And we all, when we have some years behind us and look back on life, come to realize how wise God was in not granting some of our prayers, and we may even thank him (I have done so at times) for not having listened to us when we did not know what we were asking for. Jesus himself told two of his disciples directly: "You don't know what it is you're asking." Our view of things is of necessity short, biased and selfish, and we grab impatiently the quick relief from the present pain when the true benefit for us could have been the long endurance. Most of our prayers are prayers for escape. We are afraid of suffering, and pray to be delivered from it. A sickness, a failure, a trial, a separation. We fear pain and want to be shielded from it. And God can well answer a prayer for escape with a grace to endure. Instead of removing the trial, God grants the strength to go through it; instead of levelling out the terrain, he gives the power to climb its slopes; instead of draining away our red seas, he gives us the courage to swim across them. We pray out of fear, and the right answer to the prayer is not the retreat from the threat, but the conquest of the obstacle. We do pray often with the wrong disposition, and the direction of our instinctive wishes does not coincide with that of our true welfare. Augustine was right. And then, of course, our prayer itself is not always the model prayer it

90

could be, simply because we are not ourselves the model persons we should be. Our prayer is often wanting in one or other of the four conditions listed by the manuals: attention, humility, confidence and perseverance. Yes, we pray poorly, we ask what is not good for us, and we have no merits of our own to be heard. All that is true, and goes a long way to allay our frustration when our prayers do not bring back the blessings we expected. Augustine was right. Yet, I argue on.

Those four conditions are set down in manuals of prayer, not in the Gospel. The limitations to the efficacy of our petitions were formulated by Augustine, not by Jesus. Jesus did not ask for the perfect prayer, and, if he had asked for it, he could have saved himself his trouble and his promises, because our prayers are never perfect. His promises are for the very imperfect prayer which we very imperfect people can contrive—or they are no promises at all. It is also perfectly true, of course, that we do not know what is good for us, but then since we never really know what is truly good for us, it would follow that we can never make any prayer, except, "Lord, give me what is best for me", which rather blunts the edge of petition, dilutes its urgency and makes the promises lose their boldness, and their insistence sound hollow. No. Jesus wants us definitely to ask, to ask repeatedly, to ask for concrete things, to ask for what we naively want, and to expect him to fulfill our wishes with prompt generosity. If we water down his promises, we miss something of the power of the Gospel and the depth of its message.

The answer to a mystery (and unanswered prayer is a mystery) does not lie in finding a point of equilibrium between the two extremes that appear as irreconcilable, but in holding on to both, however mutually opposed they may seem, asserting them boldly, and feeling the tension between

91

them in full sincerity and full commitment. A mystery is not a compromise between two opposites, but a committed faith in both. Three Persons in one God, God and man in Christ, bread and Presence in the Eucharist, genuine freedom of man and total dominion of God over him, goodness of God and misery of mankind—these are the great mysteries that make up human life in the wonder of its contradictions and the depth of its contrasts. And the mysteries are not to be "solved" by any mental compromise, by finding an arithmetical mean between Three and One, or a political compromise between spontaneity and predestination. No. Let the extremes stand. Bold and clear and separate. And let us proclaim both with equal conviction and determination. In the case of petitionary prayer, the extremes are God's promise and God's freedom. God's promise, by which he seems to bind himself and to place himself in our hands, and God's freedom, by which he, even after giving his promise, remains supremely independent to do his will and direct our lives holding us in *his* hands. God's promise to give us what we want, and God's freedom to do eternally what he wants. God's promise, which is familiarity and intimacy and closeness, and God's freedom which keeps him ever far and remote and transcendent. And I want to worship both. I want to receive his promises, to thank him for them, to claim them, to act on them with the certainty that God's fidelity is pledged in them and he will never let me down; and then I want to leave him free to interpret his promises as he wishes without consulting me, to react each time as he desires, to take my prayers seriously and process them at will towards whatever result he wants, sure that I will ask again and pray again and expect again... and accept his freedom again.

This discussion, though important, is getting a little too abstract, and I want to return to the concrete. I do so by remembering an episode that shook me considerably in my life, so much so that I did something unusual for me, I put down my thoughts and feelings in the shape of a letter to God and kept it with me, unposted of course; and that letter is now asking to be printed here. It speaks of itself.

"You have refused me that grace. I had asked for it repeatedly, insistently, concretely, publicly, with faith, with certainty, with enthusiasm. I was sure you wanted to give it to me now, and so had inspired me to ask for it. I had seen in it a sign of further graces. I had rejoiced in advance with my friends. And now you bluntly say No.

"I don't want to rationalize things by saying that maybe I did not pray well, or it was not expedient for me, or you are going to give me something better instead. All these things may be true (though I must say I cannot pray better and more earnestly for a thing than I have prayed for this), but I prefer just to take a straight No from you. I say it without any bad feelings. You have failed me, you have let me down, you have not fulfilled your promise. That simply means that I had not understood you and your word and your promise. That prayer is a mystery. That when I thought I knew you well, I didn't. Well, I accept you as you are, even if I don't understand you. Not that I know you better now, but at least I realize better that I don't know you. I believe in you and your word and your promise—even when I don't see how they come true. You are the Lord, you are the Master.

"Today it was hard to say the preface at Mass: 'Let us give thanks to the Lord our God'. On days when you have granted some grace I had asked for, it is so wonderful to utter those words aloud, solemnly, before all and before your altar. Today it was hard even to pronounce them. It was hard also to say the Our Father. 'Holy be your name': but

93

how can your name be holy if you don't keep your promises?

"But then at Mass I also felt a strange consolation. When holding the chalice in my hands and saying 'This is the chalice of my blood' I felt it was *my* blood, not yours, or rather mine with yours that was there. I don't want to exaggerate the disappointment of not getting that grace. In itself it is not a great thing. But the disappointment of seeing your promise fail is what hurts me. Here I am, trying to base all my life on prayer, on your promise and your power; trying to live on that and to tell others to do the same, exhorting them with your word and my experience. And the whole thing seems to fail. And I am a straight man who cannot live on make-belief. What can I do now? What can I say now? Do you understand my crisis?

"I know you understand me, because you went through a similar (only infinitely worse) disappointment in Gethsemane. You asked to be delivered from your passion. You asked the Father 'who always heard you', as you said before Lazarus' tomb, to the Father who could send twelve legions of angels to deliver you as you told Peter, you asked in the presence of three disciples (they must have heard you at least a few times before they fell asleep), you asked with full faith, and meant your prayer to be heard even if you resignedly added acceptance of the Father's will. And your prayer was not heard. You were not delivered from your passion. Not a single suffering was spared you: all the things you had announced before, that your passion would consist in, were there: spitting and scourging and insults and the cross. So may be the cross is at the heart of the mystery of unanswered prayer. As a mystery I take it. As a mystery I accept it.

94

"I know that you want me to keep asking and praying for others graces for me and for others as before, with full faith and insistence and commitment. No misgivings, no growing 'wiser' by this experience and saying, 'well, we'll keep on praying, but without banking too much on it; prayer is a good thing, but limited, and one never really knows what it is going to achieve.' No. I know that you want me to keep on praying as though nothing had happened, with full faith in your promise and in the power of prayer for all things. And so I start just now praying again.

"I will certainly tell my friends, all those who had prayed with me for this intention, that you have not granted it. I have to be honest. I pray that this may not shake their faith. There is nothing I enjoy more than praying with others for something concrete and apostolic, and seeing it happen and reporting success to you and to the group in joy and thanksgiving. And there is nothing that makes me more miserable than praying that way...and having to report to all that the prayer has failed. The worst is that this is the second time this happens to me in a short period, and my friends know it. I feel really humiliated and foolish. Maybe this is what is really hurting me, and not the fact that your promise has failed. My pride has been hurt, I have made a fool of myself before others; and then this security and guarantee of prayer I was trying to build round my life has failed, and so I feel insecure. Maybe. You may have a hundred reasons for not granting that prayer. But then, you said you would not refuse. And you have.

"This doctrine is hard, and who will take it? You remember those words, don't you? People around you said them about you, and some even left you, and you asked the Twelve whether they too wanted to go. Your sayings about your body being eaten, and your blood being drunk, were hard indeed. Hard for Peter and the Twelve too. I'm sure Peter didn't quite understand the Eucharist right at that time, didn't quite know what you were saying, but his heart was in the right place: 'Where else can we go? You only have the words of eternal life.' And so it is with me. 'Where else can I go?' I am too committed to you to go anywhere else. I am too identified with you to leave you now, even to leave you partially, to abandon this pursuit of prayer and sanctity and union and perfection, and to content myself with being a mediocre priest without going to the trouble of aspiring to higher things. No. I am with you.

"I don't even ask you to give me at once some other grace to make up for this, and to make me feel better, to show that after all you do grant graces and answer prayers. No. Have your way. Do your will. I know, even in the obscurity of this moment, that your way is true and your will is right and your power will shine through.

"I don't know what else to say. I do feel slightly better after writing this. My feelings have eased, though my hurt remains. I take you as you are, Lord. Take me as I am."

THE TRIAL OF FAITH

The reference to Gethsemane at the end of last chapter was prompted by another paragraph from C.S. Lewis which brings out, better than any other commentaries I have read, the reality of Jesus' crucial petition on earth, by emphasizing the prayer itself, not, as we usually do, the clause of submission to the Father's will that follows. "Our Lord in Gethsemane made a petitionary prayer—and did not get what he asked for. You'll remind me that he asked with a reservation—'nevertheless, not my will but thine'. This makes an enormous difference. But the difference which it precisely does not make is that of removing the prayer's petitionary character. When poor Bill, on a famous occasion, asked us to advance him a hundred pounds, he said, 'If you are sure you can spare it', and 'I shall quite understand if you'd rather not'. This made his request very different from the nagging or even threatening request which a different sort of man might have made. But it was still a request." Jesus had asked for something definite, something which meant much for him, something which he saw as possible and said so (Mk 14:36), and he had asked with the supreme confidence of the Beloved Son who is always heard by the

Father (Jn 11:42), in the agonizing insistence of a lonely night. Jesus had asked for deliverance from impending suffering and violent death. Isaac had also been brought close to death and was saved at the last moment, the obedience of Abraham being deemed sufficient sacrifice by a merciful God. Could he not, in view of his humble submission, be spared too, and the cross be avoided? He prayed in earnest for grace from his trial. Yet he was not spared. He suffered in his body the fullness of his passion, and in his heart the ultimate agony of a prayer without an answer. My Father, my Father, why have you abandoned me? The courage to pray in the face of rejection brings us close to Jesus himself in the deepest moment of his life. Every unanswered prayer is Gethsemane, and every mountain is Calvary. Faith has to be tried in order to be itself, and the greatest trial for the believer is to feel abandoned by God.

Gethsemane is the ultimate tryst for the person who prays, for the person who hopes and for the person who suffers. Suffering is the testing ground of faith, and if faith is abandoned in practice in today's world, as ever in history, the most universal reason for it is the recurring impossibility of reconciling God's existence with the sufferings of man. How can I believe in a God who makes me suffer? The wound is deep, pain breeds agnosticism, and resentment causes denial. The existence of suffering on earth is the greatest barrier against religious faith.

The riddle of human suffering, like the one of unanswered prayer of which it is only a generalization, has elicited multiple "answers", all of which have some truth in them and help up to a point in moments of trial, and all of which fall short, in fact very short, of the overwhelming reality of stark suffering in the lives of men. When suffering strikes, no argument convinces and no explanation makes sense. In fact suffering is not a problem to be discussed, but a reality, dark and painful though it is, that has to be lived. Not a notion to be grasped, but an experience to be faced. I have said that suffering can weaken faith, but that is not always so. It can even strengthen faith and lead closer to God, it can mellow tempers and deepen life, and it often does so in the secret therapy of man's lonely mind. Mahatma Gandhi compared suffering to a rope: it lifts us to God—provided we grasp it firmly with both hands. If we just hold it weakly and hesitantly, we shall slip down and fall and hurt ourselves. Suffering redeems—if we know how to hold it with a firm grasp.

Life, whatever it is, is a test, and our reactions to its vicissitudes mark the path to our future, whatever again that may be. And the test is suffering: the hardship of enduring what is not pleasant to us, and the perplexity of questioning its fairness. No promotion without test. It then follows (and here begins intellectual speculation) that, the harder the test, the higher the promotion to be expected. That is an idea I have used some times to console others, but I feel uneasy about it now. Once I told a docile audience in a family I knew well and whose members were distressed at the physical suffering that had befallen one of them, an old and saintly person of whom all spoke well and whom all loved dearly: "You see, I am a teacher, and, when I have a specially bright student, I ask him the toughest questions to give him the highest marks. That is what God is doing now with this beloved elder of yours: he is trying him harder in the last years of his life to give him a higher recompense in heaven. His sufferings now are God's testimony to him that he is a bright student, a holy soul. You may comfort yourselves and him with that thought." Well-meant words to be sure;

but, I recognize now, empty and hollow. Here, as in the twin subject of unanswered prayer and the case I mentioned there, I feel clever when I speak like that, and rather chastened and humbled when I think about it later. True, sufferings are the test and purification and expiation of faults, but it is not for me, when I am safe and contented, to tell anyone else that he is being tried for the good of his soul. We priests, professionals of condolence, are liable to treat people's sufferings lightly and officially, and fit them all nicely into the scheme of God's creation and providence which we know so well from our theology. Once a good priest whom I knew intimately, and who had gone through a long personal trial that shook him to the limits of his endurance, told me wistfully and introspectively: "One thing after this experience of mine: I will never in my life speak glibly of suffering." Beneficent lesson for all of us to learn.

The sting of suffering is not the suffering itself, painful though it be, but the realization that it has no meaning. It does not make sense, it has no explanation, it does not fit, and that hurts more than its very nails. The cross is scandal and folly, and there lies its weight. Suffering is absurd, and that is what makes it unbearable. We can walk the darkness of a tunnel if we see a light at the end of it, however tiny; but if we see no light at all, our step loses determination as we fear we are running in circles. Theilhard, in the midst of his trial of obedience, wrote poignantly: "I would drink this chalice with joy—if only I knew it was the blood of Christ." If I were sure my sufferings came from God, I would find in myself resignation to accept them. But I see them coming from the hands of violent men and senseless circumstances, and the chalice freezes in my hands. The more I reason out, the less I see. Suffering is not cured by speculation.

I am in a hospital room, sitting by the side of the bed

100

where a young girl lies with her eyes closed in sleep. I am holding her hand in mine, and I keep caressing it gently, as though to bring comfort and strength into her in her sleep before she can wake up to a new pain she does not yet know. She had been knocked unconscious, though otherwise unhurt, when a lorry without headlights had plowed blindly in the dark highway into the bus in which she was travelling at night with all her family, ripping open one side of the bus and killing all passengers sitting on that side. Her parents were among them. Even she had been sitting on the fateful side till, at the last stop, she had changed places with her brother and gone to the other side. There she had survived the impact, and is now only unconscious, mercifully sedated into blissful sleep to delay the dire awakening that will change her life. I caress her hand tenderly, fondly, desperately, while I look at her pale face, so beautiful in sleep. When she wakes up she will ask where daddy and mummy are. Their bodies are in the hospital's morgue. Who will tell her? How will she understand? Who will explain to her that she is now alone in the world, that through the mad recklessness of a drunken driver in the hostile night she has lost all her family at one stroke, and her loving parents will no more answer when she calls them? How to look at her eyes when she opens them, and meet their light and answer the question trembling in them? How to oppress her innocence with the burden of explanations she will never follow and consolations she can never understand? How to make an orphan out of a beloved daughter, a sudden adult out of a playful child? How to stay at her bedside now, waiting for that moment? But, more acutely, how to get up and steal away, leaving her to her pain, orphaned twice over in a friendless world? There is hurt in every option, and that is suffering. There is no way, no answer, no solution. There is nothing to say. The only thing to do is to press the

101

gentle hand and caress it. The only attitude before suffering is love.

The one redeeming trait of suffering is that it helps to bring out love. The pains of labour welcome the newborn into this world with the message that his mother loves him because she is willing to suffer for him. If I truly love a person, I am glad to have an occasion to suffer something for him, as a testimony and expression of my love for him. Life would be much poorer if we, indigent human beings who hardly have it in our power to do anything significant to show our concern and manifest our love, could not, at least at times, prove the sincerity of our love with the hardship of our sufferings. Here is an example of my experience which, though minimal in its value, is genuine in my private annals of friendship, and its memory gives me true inner joy even now, as did the original incident when it happened, small though it was. I wanted to see a friend in a distant town, and, when all other arrangements I tried in rural India broke down, I boarded, not without difficulty, a line bus to my destination. It boasted the ambitious denomination, "semi-luxury bus", but the luxury did not reach the dimensions of the seats nor the space between one row of seats and the next row, so that I, with my outsized legs, had to sit with my feet off the ground, my knees almost touching my chin, locked into this position from all sides by luggage, tins, bundles and people. The bus was filled beyond capacity, and the door closed with difficulty on the human cargo that occupied every available space from side to side and from engine to back. The bus started and began to make its way, the dust of the road flowing freely through the paneless windows, and the sun heating vertically our travelling furnace. The few stops the bus made offered no relief, as I found it utterly impossible to disengage myself from the solid

102

block of humanity of which I formed part for the duration of the journey. The duration was fourteen hours. They came to an end. The passengers filed slowly out of the weary bus. I was still anchored to my seat by my benumbed limbs when a well-beloved face appeared in the window near me. My friend had been waiting for me, had been alert to the arrival of the bus, and was looking for me in the dusty crowd. I do not know what I must have looked like. Dishevelled hair, contorted face, starved look, crumpled body. He saw me. He saw my plight. He saw written in my body the hardship I had endured to come to him. And his lovely face reflected in one instant pity, appreciation, pain, love and joy with such intensity that I was filled at that moment with one single irresistible feeling: blessed are these fourteen hours which by themselves have revealed my love to my friend better than a thousand words! If I had come here in a private car, at leisure by myself, it would have been fine, of course, but it would not had been clear whether what I wanted was to see my friend or to enjoy a pleasure trip in the country. Now it was clear. The luxury bus had done its job. I had cramps in my legs, and joy in my heart. And I had glimpsed the essential role of suffering, be it only the physical suffering of a harrowing journey, in telling a friend that I love him. I am reminded that God used that same language with man too. His journey to earth—and from earth—was no pleasure trip.

Audiences in Europe watched with introspective silence, which accompanied them even into the street after the show, a theatre play in which man accused and judged God for the sufferings he had inflicted on man. The prosecutor spoke of wars and violence, exile and indigence, sickness and death. The witnessess abounded in a witness-box as large as mankind. God offered no defence, gave no justification, refused to cross-examine witnesses, and stood

103

silent in expectation of the final sentence. At length man, the judge, stood up, summed up the charges, and spelled out the sentence to which he condemned God the accused. Man condemned God to be born as a man, to suffer poverty, to be driven into exile, to be misunderstood, calumniated, persecuted, to be betrayed by his own friends and abandoned by all, to be tortured in his body and to die a violent death in the flower of his life. The sentence resounded through the hall. There was silence after that. A long pregnant silence. And there the play ended. Man realized that God had already served sentence.

Suffering is a trial of faith. For a believer that trial does not lead away from God, but back again to Gethsemane, deep among the olive trees where God has come to do what he could not do in his heaven: to suffer with man. The cross of Christ is the meeting point of suffering mankind.

GLIMPSES IN THE DARK

It had been raining the whole night, and the streets in the morning were rivers of mud. I had to go over to the building across the road, and I was wondering how to make it through the impassable morass. It had stopped raining, but the mud was deep and treacherous, inviting a mishap. I came to the edge of the road, and, to my relief, I saw a line of flagstones strewn in the mud, each at some distance from the next, but close enough for a long stride to reach one at a time and make it safely to the shore. Some thoughtful person had taken trouble to place the firm stones on the muddy ground to provide a safe passage for all those who wanted to cross. I stepped gingerly on the stones. I reached the other side without difficulty. Then I looked back on the line of stones over the miry street, and I thought of a favourite idea in the realm of the spirit, a key concept to explain to myself and to others the working of faith in a world of suffering, that is its acting like glimpses in the dark, like hints in ignorance, like flagstones in the mud. Such is the concept of "sign".

A "sign" is a small reality that stands for the whole. A

105

token, a symbol, a pledge. In itself it is not much, but it points, it indicates, it signifies, and it carries within its limited boundaries the promise of an eternal reality. Such signs are abundantly given us in our exile. An inner joy, a sudden flood of peace, an intimate assurance, a sense that all is well even when nothing seems to be; meeting a kind person when all are selfish, seeing genuine concern in the midst of indifference, recognizing self-sacrifice when it seemed forgotten, detecting a gentle flower of pure innocence when all around is barren. That is the sign. Like a flash of lightning it illumines heaven and earth for a brief instant, and all is clear and beautiful and neat in its golden light. The next moment we are plunged in darkness, and in darkness we have to live and find our way—with the memory of that blessed instant to guide our steps and strengthen our heart. That is the sign. The flagstones in the mud that enable us to reach the other side when all around is danger and doubt. The mud remains, the world remains, life remains as it is with all its uncertainties and trials and sufferings; the road has not been paved and the mud has not been cleared. But a few stones wisely spaced are enough to guide a careful step. That is the sign.

Jesus did not cure all the lepers of Palestine, let alone of the whole world. He did not eradicate leprosy, nor, for that matter, any other disease. But he did cure a few lepers who came his way and asked for healing. And that is the sign. A sick man has been cured, and that means that God is here..., even if sickness continues in the world. "If I drive out devils by the Spirit of God, surely the Kingdom of God has arrived among you." (Mt 12:28). I quoted in an earlier chapter the definition of faith as believing that the Kingdom has come, in spite of all the evidence to the contrary. That adverse evidence is there, to be sure, (sickness continues), but the Kingdom is not left without its traces (a leper has been cured), and those are the "signs". Disease is the hold of sin on man's body, the grip of Satan on mortal man; and if, but once, that grip is released and the leper made clean, that is the factual announcement of the arrival of the Kingdom. That is the sign in the darkness, and that is enough to sustain faith.

Now, the sign by its very nature, is limited. It is not yet the final reality, the total victory, the new heavens and the new earth. We are still very much on the old earth, and disease is rampant and the devil is loose. But we have been given a glimpse of the reality that will one day be fully ours in glory and in splendour, and is already here with us somehow in shadow and in faith. We have been given a sign, and in the strength of it we can walk in darkness and reach in hope. The sign can be a visible sign, like a healing, or an inward one like a touch of divine consolation in prayer; it may be to an individual or to a group, it may be gentle like a breeze or overwhelming like a tempest, and in any case it is a welcome anticipation of happiness to come, a reminder, an assurance, a pledge. Signs are the fuel of our faith in our earthly journey.

Another biblical term of similar significance is "the first fruits". It was custom and law in Israel, as indeed in other agricultural tribes, to offer to God the first fruits of the land and the cattle each year, and their main religious feasts centered in fact round the seasonal ceremonies of such offerings. The gesture of offering the first fruits expressed the will of offering the whole crop to God. The first fruits were only a few ears of corn, a few grapes and dates, a basketful of fresh vegetables, but those few fruits stood for the whole harvest to come: the few in place of the whole, which is the essence of the "sign". By offering the first fruits we offer the

107

whole crop, and by offering the crop we offer ourselves. Those few ears of new corn before the altar are pledge and reminder of our own consecration to God. And so is the sign from heaven a reminder of heaven for us. The first taste of the banquet to come.

St. Paul loved that term, "first fruits", and applied it without fail to the first people he baptized in any new region, and kept calling them by that name even in later correspondence. He remembered that Epaenetus was the "first fruits" of Asia (the Roman province of Asia, Rm 16:5), and Stephanas and his family, of Achaia (1 Cor 16:15). He does not precisely mention the town, but, in both cases and significantly, the region: Asia and Achaia. Paul thought big, and when his travels took him to a new province, he thought of it as a whole, and the very first baptism in it as the "sign" that one day the whole region would accept the Gospel, as the "first fruits" of the plentiful harvest to come. When modern versions translate "Epaenetus, the first convert of Asia" they express exactly the outward meaning, while they miss the main point in Paul's expression. The "first convert" is a matter of record, a numerical first, the head of a list, long or short, which can be enlarged or may remain as it is, a mere fact without special importance; whereas the "first fruits" have necessarily to be followed by all the others of which they are symbol and representation. In baptizing its first resident, Paul baptized in hope and promise the whole region to which he belonged, and it is of that he thought from the start. In baptizing a few, Paul set up the "sign" of a Christian cell in a new territory, and moved on, sure that the "first fruits" would expand and claim the whole harvest in its day.

That outlook explains a curious word Paul uses once when reviewing his work. He writes to Rome, which he plans to visit, going against his principle to work only in places where no other apostle had yet worked, and he sums up for his new correspondents the work he has done so far, using a striking phrase: "I have completed the preaching of the Gospel of Christ from Jerusalem as far round as Illyricum." (Rm 15:19). Illyricum is Yugoslavia, and the Greek word for "completed" means, by etymology and by tense, "totally and absolutely completed", "finished up once and for ever". Paul seems to be looking at the map, taking in the whole arc of the Mediterranean (that is the "as far *round* as") from Jerusalem through the coasts and countries of Asia Minor, Greece, Yugoslavia, covering all that area with a sweep of his hand, and saying, "All this I have finished already. Now on to Rome (verse 23), and from there to distant Spain (24), and that will be all. The preaching of the Gospel will be over." He says plainly that "in these regions" (Jerusalem to Illyricum) he has finished his job and has no more scope. How could Paul, with his zeal, resources and energy, say that he had nothing more to do in the world he knew, when the vast majority of people in it had not yet even heard the message of Christ? The answer is that Paul thought in terms of "signs". It was not for him to stay in a place till it was thoroughly Christian; his responsibility was to offer the "first fruits", to set up the "sign", to sow the seed, to establish a church which, however frail, was the visible sign of the Gospel in that region—and then to move on to the next. This is all the more remarkable if we take into account that Paul expected an early second coming of Christ that would not leave much time for subsequent work. His hurry was to touch with grace all the world he knew. The Kingdom is made present by signs. Paul, the great apostle, knew it, and planed his work accordingly. He even called the risen Christ "the first fruits of the harvest of the dead" (1 Cor 15:20), because in him we too have already risen, we who have received "the firstfruits of the harvest of

109

the Spirit" (Rm 8:23), the initial grace, the pledge and guarantee of the fullness to come.

Karl Barth's commentary on "Romans" is a theological classic of the first kind, and it throws authoritative light on the point I am making here. Commenting on chapter one verse thirteen which says "I have often planned to come (to Rome) in the hope of achieving something (literally, "some little thing") among you, as I have in other parts of the world", he writes: "Whenever Paul speaks of Gentile nations and their being won for the Gospel, he always means *some few* people from those nations, as is very plain in this sentence. In those few the nations as a whole are the objects of his commission, the hearers of his message. Paul's idea of mission is not concerned with large or small numbers. What really matters is this: that the spark, and in the spark the future conflagration of the whole, is scattered throughout the world." The spark is the sign. The flag, the standard, the torch. Light it and pass it on. The first ray of the sun is the sign and assurance of the new sunrise.

Paul was a pioneer, and the "conflagration" has to follow the "spark". Still, in a way, while we are on earth we shall always depend on sparks, as the final conflagration will be only at the end of time. On earth we always live on faith, and faith operates through signs. The triumphalism of numbers made us almost believe once that the Kingdom was already visible on earth, that the Gospel had already been preached to every creature, that the Church was already factually universal. Sober reality teaches us to see that in the confusion and indifference of the modern world we are still a minority, we are still a "little flock", the "remnant of Israel", a "diaspora Church"— which are all biblical terms and historical realities. We are ourselves a sign to the world. We

110

are small, and the strength of our faith has to make up for the frailty of our condition.

In the idea and the practice of the sign we find the balance between over-enthusiam on one side, and despair on the other: the despair that says "we can do nothing", and the over-optimism that would push us to do everything as though the total welfare of the whole of mankind were to be achieved by us here and now. Both extremes are seriously harmful, and the centre between them lies in the sign. The sign has to be clear and sharp and distinct for all to see, and so we will work with all zeal and enthusiasm to be the sort of persons we ought to be and to reach out to as many people as we can with the sincerity of our love and the totality of our efforts; but then, the sign is only a sign, and so we will not lose our peace or let our minds be upset when we see that the darkness continues all around us and the world goes very much its own way in spite of all our efforts. The consciousness of being a sign reconciles within our hearts zeal with patience, optimism with realism, faith with facts. Jesus himself had felt within himself the impatience to undergo the final "baptism with which I have to be baptized", together with the resignation to wait for the times "which the Father has kept in his own reckoning". The theology of the sign is as practical in its applications as it is rich in its meaning.

I heard a zealous priest say: "I will give myself no rest so long as there is a hungry man in my parish." Those were beautiful words of a priest who loved his people, felt their sufferings as his own, and had pledged himself to do all he could to alleviate them. That is Christian love, concern for the poor and dedication to their uplift. I would like for myself the burning zeal and the untiring efforts of that holy priest before whom I bow my head. At the same time, however, I feel uneasy when I hear him speak like that, I sense he is overstraining himself in actual work and in keeping up a supporting ideology for his exertions, and I fear his zeal may bring frustration and defeat itself in the long run, which, perhaps, may not be so very long either. For one thing, his parish is very large, there are many thousands in it who live below the poverty line, and it seems to me a practical impossibility for him with any resources to achieve sufficiency for all in any foreseeable future. Even if he does, there are many more poor people, neighbouring the boundaries of his parish, who live in the same plight, and who will also claim his attention and defeat his personal rest if he turns to them after redeeming his first poor. And then, and this is my main consideration, this attitude of totality, of planning for redemption in one's lifetime, of wanting to do everything, even if that everything is something so legitimate and necessary as the eradication of hunger from a district, of committing oneself to a concrete result and vowing no quarter till it is achieved, can deviate from the right attitude which, while endeavouring by all possible means to serve others and relieve misery and achieve results, realizes and accepts its own limited role in a vast world, and rests at peace in the real, though partial, value of its own witnessing. We are not to take the witness for the whole case, the sign for the totality, nor ourselves for almighty God. It was a Pope, Pius XII, who liked to remind his own staff: "We are not the Divine Providence." Neither are we.

I again heard a holy and revered social worker say in public: "Why to speak of a problem of abortion in the world? Give those children to me; I will look after them." The gesture of love, the concern for the unborn child, the readiness to help, backed unmistakeably by a life of heroic work and total dedication to the most derelict causes in humanity, are genuine and touching, and merit my whole appreciation and admiration. When, however, I heard those words, I felt a gentle jarring inside me, and I allowed my own critical mind to lay its objection before me. A problem of abortion does exist, and is worldwide. The problem is not only the care of the unwanted child, but has other obvious aspects with no ready solution. Even the single aspect of the care of the child is wider than any one person or institution could contemplate for a total solution. And then, and this is again my main point, in taking that attitude we are mistaking the sign for the totality, the pointer for the destination, the redeeming gesture for the overall solution of a worldwide problem. To take care of all the unwanted children in the world is plainly impossible; on the other hand, to save even one such child, to take in one's loving arms an abandoned infant, to nurse it, to give it a home and a future is one of the loveliest works man can do, and one which, apart from saving the child, gives ailing mankind the joy to see that there is still goodness among men, and the right to hope in the midst of a forlorn world. To save one such child is not only an act of love for him, but for mankind, and so its incalculable value stands—even if the problem of abortion remains. That is the sign. And what is beautiful as a sign, can sound pretentious if proposed as a universal remedy. To sum up clearly: the fact that one child is saved brings hope for mankind, and the more such children are saved, the better; still the problem will remain—and so of all problems in our troubled world. Our effort for solutions has to be unremitting; while our acquiescence in reality remains unchallenged. Happy is he who combines realism and idealism in his life. What I am saying in this chapter is that the notion of "sign" helps us to do that.

I have used the notion of "sign" with some effectiveness

113

to help young men when they come into life, and the winds of the world hit them, and their optimism withers in one night, and they pass suddenly from the generous ambition to set right in record time all that is wrong with the world, to the total despair that nothing can be done about anything, and the only way out is to join the defaulting crowds and cheat one's way through life as all miserably do. When a young man loses his ideals he loses them thoroughly, and crosses over to the camp of the disillusioned, bag and baggage. Then he can be told gently: Yes, many cheat and many lie and give and take bribes. But not all. Even in the darkest days of Israel's history there were some who "had not bent their knee to Baal". There are students who do not cheat in the examination, and officials who do not accept bribes. That is what I call a witness, a pointer, a sign. A ray of light in the darkness, a bird's song in the desert, a reminder of hope. The honest behaviour of one such person in the middle of corruption and graft is a practical and effective way of saying that not all is lost in the battle of virtue, and that one can still be honest and succeed in life. In a word, that one can still be a "sign" — and that is the greatest service he can render to himself and to society.

The idea of "sign" has also helped me to understand situations, even outside purely religious activities, which make sense in this context, and lose all credibility if taken out of it. I give a clear example: The *Bhoodan* ("land-gift") movement of Acharya Vinoba Bhave. That saint of modern India conceived a plan to ease the basic tension in rural areas between the few zamindars (landlords) and the many landless labourers. He walked on foot from village to village, and appealed directly to those who owned large properties of land to donate part of them, which he later would distribute among those who owned nothing. The scheme

114

was simple, its need glaring, and the saintliness and persuasiveness of the Acharya were guarantee of efficiency and fairness. Many lands were donated and distributed. Some observers were led to believe that here was the solution to India's economic problems. The majority of India's poor live in the villages; give each a piece of land, and they will all have enough to eat and to live. Enthusiasts of *Bhoodan* spoke exaltedly and convincingly during the years the movement was gathering momentum and claiming attention. They saw in it the moral and practical force that was going to change the face of India in a matter of years, and they had some apparent reasons to believe so. They were, however, disappointed. A number of selfless workers dedicated themselves to the cause; books were written and weekly papers in several languages printed. But no practical results were forthcoming at any noticeable level. And here again sceptics and critics seized the statistics and pronounced the whole movement a total failure. Both extremes were wrong, and, to my mind, the right evaluation of this important campaign hinges on the value and the concept I am enlarging upon in this chapter. As a call to awareness in an urgent cause, as an object lesson, as a dramatized appeal, as an imaginative campaign of general concientization, as a token, as an image, as a sign, Vinoba's gesture to me was a stroke of genius, and his venerable figure walking the parched landscape in graphic apostolate became a source of hope and faith and inspiration to millions in India. On the other hand, as a remedy to India's economic woes, *Bhoodan* was a failure. The "sign" changes the heart, not the situation; gives hope, not solutions; is a morning ray, not the noonday sun. And, here again, it is mistaking the sign for the whole that brings confusion, disillusionment and frustration, as it did even among some of the followers of the Acharya. His work was splendid, even through the practical results were limited.

115

Problems are always going to remain in our wide world. Let us by all means and in every way contribute all we strenuously can to solve them, remembering at the same time that what most of us can do is barely a drop in the ocean—but a drop that counts, if we understand its nature and appreciate its value. The kind hand that laid the flagstones in the mud.

THIS WILL BE YOUR SIGN

All signs derive their meaning from Jesus, the perfect sign. He was limited in space and time. A short span of life in a reduced extension of land. He was sent only "to the lost sheep of the house of Israel"; he hardly ever crossed its boundaries, and rarely spoke with foreigners. The angel instructed the shepherds: "This will be your sign." A sign to find the Sign. A crib and swaddling clothes. Sings of poverty to find the King. A small child, but in him the Kingdom has arrived. "He who sees me, sees the Father." The infiniteness of God in the concreteness of a man, a few years that span eternity, a limited presence that fills creation. If the Son of Man can make the Father present, so can we, in our smallness and poverty, reflect his glory till he comes. We are signs in the Sign.

Jesus performed "signs". He resented at times being asked to do so, but that was only when he was asked as a challenge to prove himself, or as a curiosity to entertain the crowds, or, more insultingly, as a spectacle to please a king who could send him to his death. And he was asked, sometimes very rudely, precisely because he was known to

117

have the power to perform them. Jesus himself summed up his activities in a report he meant to reach the ears of Herod: "Today and tomorrow I shall be casting out devils and working cures; on the third day I reach my goal." (Lk 13:32). He chose disciples "to be with him, to be sent to proclaim the Gospel and to drive out devils" which, in Mark's language, means healing the sick (Mk 3:14). His disciples were even to perform greater deeds than he (Jn 14:12), and that was in fact the way the message spread: "The whole company fell silent and listened to Barnabas and Paul as they told of all the signs and miracles that God had worked among the Gentiles through them." (Ac 15:12).

The healing, the cure, the stilling of the storm, the feeding of the crowd are "signs" in the perfect sense of the word. They point to a presence while they, by themselves, do not compel submission. Some saw and believed. Many others saw them and remained unmoved. Still others saw them and became violent. "What action are we taking? This man is performing many signs. If we leave him alone like this the whole populace will believe in him." (Jn 11:47). Jesus was killed because of his signs. And the painful reality was no surprise. His own mother had heard the prophecy: "This child is destined to be a sign of contradiction. Many in Israel will stand or fall because of him." The sign is a challenge, and brings about decision—for or against, in man's freedom and the mystery of grace. The sign heals, and who would not like to be healed? But in healing, the sign brings man face to face with a power greater than himself, and man resents anything that disturbs his mental routine, his own comfortable way of looking at things and understanding life. The man blind from birth to whom Jesus gave sight was overjoyed to be able to see and to move and to be free from the opprobrium and the suffering he had endured from his birth. His parents, however, were alienated, avoided questions, refused to get involved. And the Pharisees became bitter and swore hatred. Around a sign there is always a growing circle of uneasiness, resistance, opposition. Man resents the interference of the divine in his well-calculated world.

Once Jesus healed a madman who went about naked and broke chains, and the people of his village came to see back in his senses a man whose plight had been for years the talk of the village. They saw him, they verified his sanity, and then they went to Jesus and placed a special request before him: Please, go away. "The whole population of the Gerasene district asked him to go." (Lk 8:37). That was not precisely because, as a result of the event, a herd of pigs had been lost over the cliff in the lake, but because "seeing the man from whom the devils had gone out sitting at Jesus' feet clothed and in his right mind, they were afraid." "They were in the grip of a great fear." They felt uneasy in the presence of a new power, they did not want the trouble of having to assimilate a new situation, the risk of having to change. They anticipated new demands in the impressive authority that had crossed their frontiers, and they did not want to have to adjust to them. They acted quickly and in a body. "The routine of life had been unsettled and disturbed, and they wanted the disturbing element removed as quickly as possible. The one battle-cry of the human mind is 'Please, don't disturb me'. On the whole, the one thing that people want is to be let alone. The Gerasenes banished the disturbing Christ—and still men seek to do the same." (Barclay). Then Jesus "got into the boat and returned." He left without a word. He did not impose himself. The sign was there—to stand or to fall by, to accept or to reject. The sign is only a sign: it shows the way and it respects freedom. It seems likely

119

that Jesus had intended to stay in the region of the "Ten Towns" to preach the Gospel there, because he did a rather unusual thing with the healed man: instead of imposing silence on him, as was Jesus' usual practice after a healing, this time, on the contrary, he positively asked the beneficiary of the miracle, who wanted to go with him, to stay back among his own people and tell them his story. "The man went off and spread the news in the Ten Towns of all that Jesus had done for him". Jesus left there a sign to speak for him, but he withdrew. The Gerasenes quickly converted the episode into a memory of the past, a legend in the village folklore. Life went on as usual in the Ten Towns. Routine had been saved—and people love routine.

Faith is never comfortable; it is no bed of roses, no leisurely insurance. Faith is the capacity to be disturbed, to let God into one's life, to cope with the unusual and to be surprised into glory. And faith is, in turn, the capacity to disturb others, not in the obnoxious pride of inconsiderate manners, but in the humble role of carriers of faith, of secondary signs that reflect with delegated light the presence and the demands of the One Sign. We too, when we act in Jesus' name, are signs of contradiction as he was, and bear the responsibility of eliciting reactions to him through us. When a priest, a religious, a person of faith walks into society, into a group of friends, into a family, into a man's life, he brings with him the values he represents, the truths he believes and the attitudes he defends. He stands in the name of Jesus. He walks the streets of today's world the way Jesus walked the streets and roads and market places of his world, and becomes a sign for men to react to. A religious person is a sign in the midst of society. "He who hears you, hears me."

King Ahab resented the very existence of the prophet Elijah, and when the prophet walked on his own into his presence, the king greeted him with royal scorn: "Here is the troubler of Israel!" (1 Kg 18:17). No better compliment could Elijah have chosen for himself. He was the conscience of Israel. His very presence reminded a wanton king of his infidelity and injustice. Before Elijah could open his mouth (he had come in fact to offer rain in the name of God over a parched kingdom) the king expressed his displeasure because Elijah stood for the God he had rejected. A man of God brings judgement into the world by his very presence. "He who receives you, receives me." The sign of contradiction is a sign of judgement.

The sign does not cause judgement as a judge would do by hearing a cause and pronouncing sentence, but by letting the person react to it spontaneously... and allowing that reaction to speak by itself. When I was studying music, my teacher was one day playing in class something on the piano for our comments and appreciation, and one of the students told him, "Please, sir, play something else; what you are playing now is boring." The teacher interrupted his playing, turned to the student who had passed that remark, and said in a sad voice: "What I was now playing was Beethoven; and if you are in this class and you don't like Beethoven, you have defined yourself." Nobody has condemned you; you have condemned yourself by the way you have reacted. Beethoven does not stand on judgement, you do. "I do not judge anyone", said Jesus, and yet he is judge of the living and the dead. Men are judged by the way they react to him. He was the perfect sign, the sign of contradiction, or, as Guillet translates, the "object of discernment" that brings out what is in man by appearing before him and letting him define himself. If the Gerasenes asked Jesus to go away, the Samaritans, confronted with another sign reported by one of their women at the well

121

("he has told me everything I ever did"), were not afraid to take into their midst one who could read their hearts, and asked him insistently to come to their village and stay with them. Jesus went and stayed with them two days. Many believed in him.

THE SIGN OF JOHN

There was a man sent by God. His name was John. He was not the light, but he came to bear witness to the light. He himself was a sign, in his life and in his message, of the Sign that was to come "to lay bare what was in the hearts of men". The birth of John was attended by "signs", and people began to wonder. "All their neighbours were filled with awe, and the whole affair was talked about throughout the hill country of Judaea. All those who heard of it treasured it in their hearts. What will this child turn out to be? they wondered. And the hand of the Lord was with him."

John was a child when all that happened, but as he grew up he must have learned of the events that surrounded his birth, and they moulded his life from childhood. Why he was called John instead of Zechariah like his father, why he was never given wine or cider, why all treated him differently from other boys, why he was drawn to live in the desert, why he felt called to a role he did not quite know but would find out as he went along.

He did not know who it was he had to announce (Jn 1:33), nor when he would appear, yet he opened in faith an

Advent of hope for Him who was to come. He preached, he admonished, he even expressed the urgency of his message in the public gesture of a visible rite and he went down into the waters of the river and washed with them, in fact and figure, the men and women whom his austerity attracted and inspired to purify themselves for the coming visitation. It must have taken faith to say, "He is coming" when he did not know when he was to come or how he himself was to know, nor indeed what the exact identity was of the person whose sandals he would not be worthy to unfasten. Yet he went on with his announcing and he gathered the crowds and demanded penance. Prepare the way. Someone is coming, and the coming will make all the difference to the world. Wait for him. He is coming.

He came. John was told: the one on whom you see the Spirit rest, he is the expected one, the one you are announcing. John saw him and saw the Spirit. And from that moment the whole of John was a single gesture with his outstreched arm and his constant declaration: There he is! He is the one of whom I spoke, the one for whose arrival I asked you to purify yourselves, the one who will baptise you with fire and the Holy Spirit. Go to him.

"The next day he saw Jesus coming towards him. 'Look', he said, 'there is the Lamb of God; it is he who takes away the sin of the world. This is he of whom I spoke when I said, "After me a man is coming who takes rank before me"; for before I was born, he already was. I myself did not know who he was; but the very reason why I came, baptizing in water, was that he might be revealed to Israel.' " (Jn 1:29-31).

John's mission was to turn people towards Jesus. "There is the Lamb of God." The witness, the testimony, the appeal. Follow him. Go and see. Find out for yourselves.

Just go near him and speak with him and let yourselves be guided by what he speaks to you. Once you are in contact with him, my work is over. I have made disciples only in order that they may become his disciples. I have told people to be honest, so that they could now face him and meet his gaze. I have straightened the roads for people to travel and come to him. That is my mission. That is my life.

Some even complained to John that Jesus made more disciples than he did, and that his own disciples were leaving him to go to Jesus. That was precisely what John wanted to do: make people go to Jesus. Yet there is a human touch in his reaction, a wistful comment in which he accepts the privilege of being a "sign", while at the same time recognizing its limitation, which almost hurt: "A man can have only what God gives him." (Jn 3:27). He is not the Messiah but his forerunner, not the bridegroom, but the bridegroom's friend; but then, beautifully, "the bridegroom's friend stands by and listens to him, and is overjoyed at hearing the bridegroom's voice." Always discreet, always at a distance, always ready to be eclipsed, to "diminish as he increases". That is the very definition of the sign: to point out, to prepare, to rejoice..., and then to disappear. That is the vocation of John.

John knew his mission well, and he also knew it was hard, and found it so himself as he advanced in it. He had boldly proclaimed that he had to diminish, and he found himself in jail, forgotten except by a group of devoted disciples, and threatened by the whims of a debauched king. Jail was hard, solitude was trying, and more trying was the doubt that tortured him day and night in the long hours of his dark dungeon: Was what he had lived for actually true? Was his call genuine and his mission authentic? Is Jesus truly the Messiah? Nothing seems to happen of all that I predicted.

125

I proclaimed that the axe was already laid to the root, that the shovel was ready in his hand, and he would winnow his threshing-floor to gather the wheat into his granary, and to burn the chaff in a fire that would never go out. But nothing of the kind has happened or seems about to happen. Society goes its way as before, Jesus just moves around, I, his herald, am in jail, and wicked courtiers rule the wishes of the king. Could it be that this was not the true Messiah, that I mistook the signs, that I in my impatience got the wrong person and misled the people? Could it be that the true Messiah is still to come, and we all have to wait for him, for the new man to bring about the renovation I have announced?

That is the trial of faith of every apostle. I have proclaimed the Kingdom, I have encouraged people, I have assured them that truth always wins, that honesty is the best policy, that God is just and the Gospel is true; I have built up faith and inspired love, I have declared that prayers are heard and virtue is rewarded, I have announced the presence of the one who comes to baptise in fire and the Spirit. And when after many years of hard work and unremitting labours I soberly sit down and look around and examine the results and watch the facts and search my soul with searing sincerity, I feel the darkness of John's dungeon all around me, and his question becomes mine. Is this what I've been working for? Is this what I've lived for? Was all I've proclaimed worth all my efforts and my labours and my life? Or have I missed the point somewhere, have I deluded myself, have I followed a shadow and is all darkness now? Where is the fire and the Spirit? Where is the Gospel and the Kingdom? It's been a long road and I see close the end of my years—without the light I expected before the end. Nothing has happened. Nothing has changed. I'll leave the world as I found it. I'll waste my life to the end as I've wasted

126

it so far. What, then, of my hope? What of my testimony? What of the one who was to come?

John in his anguish asked the question, and asked it of Jesus himself. If Jesus was not the one who was to come, at least he would know, at least John could learn something from his answer, since he could not expect help from anywhere else in the solitude of his dungeon and in the depth of his doubt. He desperately wanted reassurance and expected it from the naked question that gnawed at his heart. He managed to contact two of his disciples whom he could trust, and charged them to go to Jesus and ask him the straight question: "Are you the one who is to come, or are we to wait for someone else?" Tragic question for a man to ask from a dungeon he is not to leave alive. Was I right in pointing to you, or have I still to look for another, when I don't know how long I will be able to look at all? There is pathos in that question, and the whole life of John is in it. It would be naive to take John's question as a teaching device to make his disciples get an answer from Jesus for their benefit while he, John, knew fully well the answer and was only feigning ignorance. That would be unworthy of the seriousness of the moment. Nobody plays games from a cell in jail, and John and Jesus were not playing a game. John was in dead earnest. He asked because he needed to know, he needed to know before he died that his life had not been in vain, that his prophecy had not remained in the air, that his mission had not been a failure. And it is to him that Jesus' answer is directed: "Go and tell John." He needs the answer. Make your way back to the dungeons of Herod and let John know.

John's idea of the Kingdom was quite different from that of Jesus. And that is also the trouble with us. We want results, we want the temporal kingdom, the political victory, the shaking off of the Roman yoke, we want tangible sanctity, we want recognition, we want success. We have our own idea of what the Kingdom of God should be in the world and in our souls, and we work to build up our own model, only to be disappointed when we see it does not work. And then we wonder. We thought we knew, and we find we do not. That finding is painful. John had reproached the Jews: "In the midst of you there is one you do not know." And now, pathetically, he is made to realize that he himself does not know Jesus. He had assumed Jesus would think as he thought, he had projected his own dreams on Jesus, he had taken Jesus for granted. And that is the greatest mistake man can ever make. Jesus is different, and his freedom strains our expectations. His answer reached John back in the solitude of his trial of faith.

"Go and tell John: the blind see, the lame walk, the lepers are made clean, the deaf hear, the poor have the Good News announced to them...; and happy is he who does not lose faith over me!" Those words were straight for John. Happy will you be if you do not lose faith in me till the end, whatever may happen. True, the signs are there. John, the sign, being himself in need of "signs". The blind, the deaf, the dead. All that is reassuring. But, if he can do all that, why cannot he set me free from my prison? Why have I to be satisfied with a second-hand account of wonders that do not affect me, while I am deprived of the one favour I would personally appreciate? Why has the Kingdom to be manifested in a blind man's eyes and not in a prisoner's freedom? What Kingdom is this that allows the one who ushered it in to languish in prison? Why does he talk in riddles to me? Why does he not answer my question straight? Is he or is he not? He only tells me not to lose faith in him. At least he knows well what my real problem is. Can I still trust him in the face of total disappointment?

128

Words for John. Words for us. Happy is he who does not lose faith over me. Do not lose faith. Not even in darkness. Not even in a dungeon. Not even when a henchman comes with orders from a king and wishes from a dancing girl and the vengeance of a concubine, and there is a sword in his hands, and a platter in the hands of a slave who follows to receive and exhibit before drunken guests the head of the prophet. Do not lose faith. Hold on. I was he who was to come. Your life is what was to have been, the world is what God meant it to be, and you yourself, however much of a puzzle you may be to yourself, are also God's beloved son, accepted and honoured in his own household.

Are you the one who is to come? My question. With my life in it. Is this what I had to expect? Is this what I have fought for? Is this what the Gospel means? Is this the Church? Is this the Kingdom? With the sincerity of a man who sees death from a dungeon, I confess that what I see does not adjust itself to my idea of what should be. My Messiah was different. My dream was of another world. And yet, with the final commitment of my last breath in a dark prison, I proclaim my faith and swear my allegiance.

It was only when John's messengers had left the presence of Jesus and were out of hearing that Jesus began to praise John at length before all present, as he never did with anyone else in his life. And in his praises, a telling image: John was not a reed bent by the wind. He was firm and steady, and Jesus publicly proclaimed his unique role in preparing his coming. Yes, Jesus was he who was to come, and John was his herald. "He is the man of whom Scriptures says: Here is my herald whom I send on ahead of you, and he will prepare your way before you." Clear words, which the messengers were not to report.

John dies, witness and martyr, in the darkness of his royal prison and in the darkness of his trial of faith. He never heard the words of the Master: "I assure you that no mother's son on earth is greater than John the Baptist."

ON MOVING MOUNTAINS

Treating of faith includes treating of charismatic faith, however risky the theme may be, and I am going to do it in my own way in this chapter. It will be made up of three experiences, simply and objectively narrated. I begin it with the resolution to let the three stories stand by themselves without commentary, and with the fear that I shall not be able to overcome the temptation to add my totally unnecessary remarks at the end, and I shall spoil their effect with my officiousness. Why cannot I trust my readers to draw by themselves the balanced non-credulous non-sceptical impression which the selection and telling of the three experiences sufficiently create by themselves? Miracles can happen, and miracles need not be miracles, though God's love and care shine through every circumstance he chooses to act through. The hand of the Lord has not been shortened; he can and does exercise his power in ways beyond our ways, and even when he works through means we understand, his message of hope can be read in his doings by those who believe in his love and have faith in his power. As I write this I feel myself the curiosity to know what I shall actually do at the end of the chapter. I shall have to wait and see. Meanwhile here are the stories.

131

First. It is Pentecost day. I am concelebrating a solemn Mass of the Holy Spirit together with a large number of priests, to mark the end of a meeting that has kept us busy for a week with discussions and papers and resolutions and all the standard folklore such meetings happily and harmlessly entail. I love the careful liturgy of the meaningful Mass, and at the same time I realize with a touch of remorse that my mind is not fully in it. After the Mass I have to dash to the airport to catch a plane, and I am keeping an eye on my watch, anxious that the unfolding of the rubrics may not reduce the narrow margin between the last blessing and the take-off. So far the service proceeds smoothly. The ever surprising story of the first Pentecost in Acts, the verses on the Holy Spirit that make me remember nostalgically the beauty of their now remote Latin original, the promise of the divine Helper in the Gospel, a pointed homily full of learned fervour, and then prayers for all and for ourselves, for the work we have planned these days and the fruit of our efforts in the future. I am now reading aloud the eucharistic prayer in unison with all the priests around the altar. It is then that I notice one thing. I am crying. Big tears are rolling down my cheeks, and I have to draw quickly a handkerchief to prevent them from dropping on to the liturgical booklet in my hand. I am surprised at the tears, and surprised at the fact that there has been no feeling before them, no emotional state that may have preceded them. It is not any feeling that has induced the tears, but the opposite, the tears that after flowing in abundance are now bringing with themselves a current of feeling that begins to fill my soul with an intensely pleasurable violence. I cannot read the book, I cannot speak, I hardly know where I am, only that everything around is beautiful and glorious and angels are singing and stars are shining and I am full of a heavenly bliss which eye has not seen and heart has not felt and words cannot describe. I follow the Mass more alert than ever through the mist of my tears. I approach the altar for communion with a reverence that melts my heart, almost feeling in my body the very presence of the divinity. I sit down again at my place in the middle of continuing bliss. I keep wiping away tears. And then I remember. Nine days earlier I had finished with a group of friends a deep spiritual experience. We had spent one month together in total silence and constant prayer in a selected spot in Khandala up in the slopes of the Western Ghats between Bombay and Poona, and on the last day of the deep spiritual renewal we had agreed, when parting company, to pray for each other for the nine days that remained till the feast of Pentecost, asking that each one of us should receive that day the Holy Spirit in a special way. I had in fact prayed each day, and I believed in prayer, chiefly prayer for one another, prayer repeated day after day, prayer for the gift of gifts which the Father is eager to grant to those who ask him. Yet I was entirely unprepared for a tangible, experienceable, overpowering manifestation of the gift. When I saw the connexion, I smiled to myself between my tears. Had I not asked for it? So there it was. Prayer worked after all, and the Spirit had kept his date. I had at times said in spiritual talks that tears are the visiting card of the Holy Spirit. Now I knew it. Unmistakeable identity. No one else could have done that to me. Not in that way. My soul was stirred to its very depths. That was some Pentecost for me.

In the midst of that bliss I did not forget the practical world. The Mass was over. I checked my watch. There was just time. I grabbed my luggage, hailed a taxi, jumped into it and reached the airport. I was deeply calmed, and the tears had ceased. I entered the airport, went to the counter, checked in, learned that my flight was delayed, and sat down for lunch at the airport restaurant. My lunch was over and the flight was announced. I boarded the plane, chose a window seat and noticed with satisfaction that the seat next to mine remained empty. After take-off I called the stewardess and instructed her not to bring anything to me or disturb me in any way, as I wanted to sleep. And so I honestly had meant to do. But I did not succeed. The tears started again, and with them the onslaught of joy. This time even stronger than on the ground. I kept looking ahead of me, dazed with heavenly delight, making now no attempt to wipe the tears that flowed freely and abundantly down my whole face. Then I realized that the stewardess had noticed me and my situation. She was looking at me, hesitating about what to do. I must have looked quite a sight, a mature man, a priest if she had rightly interpreted the cross on my lapel, weeping uncontrollably in an airplane seat with the seat-belt on. That was surely a new item in the variegated experience of an air hostess. Not in the manual, I guess. She went up the aisle, and I saw her speak to the male steward. Then both came to me together, the man bent towards me very gently as the girl looked on, and asked me: "Are you unwell? Can we do anything for you?" Pretty plight I was in. How to tell them it was Pentecost, and one could expect such things to happen on that day? I just smiled my help-lessness through my tears. They brought me a glass of water, and compassionately watched me drink it. I thanked them and assured them I was fine. They withdrew and kept watching me at intervals. The flight continued. It took me to Bombay where I had to change planes to reach my final destination, Ahmedabad. I sat in the new plane, and the tears came again. It was still Pentecost. I finally reached my place, and found there one of those companions who had been with me in the prayer experience at Khandala for the whole month, and was also therefore in the prayer pact that followed it. I literally assaulted him, caught both his shoulders in both my hands, shook him bodily and asked him almost aggressively: "Did anything happen to you today?" He took the attack gamely and answered: "Not till you came in!" Then I told him my story. He had prayed daily for me those nine days, and I assured him his prayer had been heard. For months after that day I lived in heaven. The tears did not come again, but their effect was deep and lasting. I knew from books that God can act directly on the soul. Now I could quote day and hour—and flight number.

Second. I am conducting a thirty-day retreat for priests. We are in the first days, and I don't yet know my men, when I am informed that the doctor has had to be called in to see one of them. I ask to see the doctor and listen to his report. One of the priests is confined to bed. Spine trouble. The doctor tells me he will not be able to get up for the whole month, even if he wants to, and a severe treatment with an eventual operation is the only hope if ever he is to move freely again. As for these thirty days now, the doctor, who knows the nature of our spiritual experience, advises that, since the patient can read and pray, he could be allowed to follow the group from his sick-bed, and thus fulfill the requirement of the month of prayer, together with the discomfort of his illness. I readily agree, and the day goes on. At night, the last item in the day, we all meet together in the chapel for an hour-long uncharted prayer. Anyone in it is free to contribute his thoughts or mention his desires before God and the group. In that prayer that day I mention the sick man and pray for his recovery. I do it because I know I am expected to do it. I know I am the leader of the group, a member is sick, so the proper thing for me to do is to mention it in the group prayer that closes the day and to ask that he may be healed. I do so, and I do it without real faith, without personal commitment, without urgent concern. Purely official prayer. I know how to word it effectively, and I do so in the darkened chapel. The prayer fills the silence for a while. Others too pray. One of them makes a reference in his prayer to something I had said that day in a talk to the group. The next day was to be confession day, when we all were recommended to cleanse our souls in the sacrament of reconciliation to open up the channels of grace for each other and for the group in those days of prayer. I had mentioned the Gospel scene where Jesus cures a paralytic, and explicitly makes the healing of his body an external sign of the healing of his soul saying, "To convince you that the Son of Man has the right on earth to forgive sins... stand up (he said to the paralytic), take your bed and go home." So this man who is praying now after me in the intent group, quotes the Gospel, quotes me who quoted it in the context of tomorrow's confessions, and draws the conclusion of the quotation in the simplicity of his faith: "Tomorrow, Lord, we, your priests, are going to your sacrament of pardon to open our souls to you and to your grace and to your Spirit. One of our brothers is sick, so sick that he cannot come here to pray with us, and so we bring him to you here in spirit, as the friends of that paralytic brought him to you. Heal him in his body with your power, that we may know in truth that you are healing us in our souls through your sacrament when we receive it tomorrow." That is his prayer. I frown in the darkness, as it seems to me too bold to be made in public. A few more pray. Then silence. The day is over.

The next day I take my chair punctually for the morning talk I give each day to the whole group together to focus the day and help the prayer. In the group I seem to recognize the sick man. Or am I mistaken? I ask no questions. Later in the morning I go to his room as though to visit him and inquire about his health. He is the man. I sit by his side and, uneasy to ask, keep silent. He understands and speaks slowly. "Yesterday I couldn't move. Any attempt to change position in bed brought on unbearable pain. At night I couldn't sleep at first, then somehow I fell asleep. When I woke up I waited for the pain, but it did not come. I ventured to move a little in bed, and I found I could do it easily. I felt normal all over, and so when the time for your talk came and I heard the bell, I got up and walked up the stairs and went to the hall and sat for the length of your talk. And here I am." He is so matter-of-fact that there is nothing for me to say. The doctor sees him later and shrugs his shoulders. In the group prayer at night, with the cured man present, I thank the Lord for hearing our prayers and confirming once more the grace of the sacrament with the sign of his healing. The group takes it all in its stride. They already live in an atmosphere where everything is possible. Even for a serious spine ailment to disappear overnight and never to come again. Personally I feel chastened. Every time I see that man I feel a sense of reverence as I would feel before a place or an object on which the hand of the Lord had rested. A eucharistic feeling. He never mentions the matter again. Nobody else does. I do not even know to this day who made the faith-filled prayer that brought healing. In the darkness of the chapel I had not seen him, and I did not recognize his voice. God did.

Third. I am in Nairobi taking leave of the Indian friends who had invited me to Kenia for religious talks and meetings with them for a few days that had proved a truly happy and inspiring time for me. They have come to the airport to see me off. From Nairobi I am going to Dar-es-Salaam for a similar programme. At the airport there is the confusion of the farewells and of the many travellers who crowd the counters at the time, as there are two flights to the same destination starting within an hour of each other. The first is my flight. It is direct, non-stop, and will take me to Dar-es-Salaam in time for my first public talk which the organizers have fixed and announced for this evening, as it is Sunday when all can come and the lecture series can get off to a good start. The second flight starts later and has two stops on the way, arriving in Dar-es-Salaam at night. I have made sure my ticket is for the first flight, I have cabled my hosts in Dar-es-Salaam, and they will be waiting for me at the airport, welcome relief when landing for the first time in a new country. I go through the formalities, book my two bags, get my boarding pass, and take leave with gratitude of the many friends who have stayed with me till the last moment. And now I am alone in the last waiting hall. My flight is announced. I join the queue to file out onto the tarmac, and show my boarding pass confidently at the gate. The airline girl looks at it, stops me and says politely: "Your flight is the next one. Please wait in the hall. You'll leave in an hour's time." I look with horror at my boarding card. She is right. The number on it, bold and clear, is the number of the next flight that starts an hour later and goes round and has two stops and reaches at night. I am stranded. I realize what has happened. The girl who checked me in at the counter was handling both flights, she had mixed the flights up and, though my ticket was for the first flight, she had mistakenly placed me and my luggage in the wrong one, giving me the wrong boarding pass. I, unforgivably, had taken the boarding pass without looking at it, and here I was now in a real quandary. I shall reach late, I may find nobody at the airport, I shall miss my first talk; and in being inconvenienced myself, I shall inconvenience everybody else. Fine way to set foot in a new country! I feel so desperate that I plead with the girl: "Listen. You are right. My boarding pass is for the next

138

flight. But this is a mistake. I know I meant to go by the first flight. If there is place in the plane, please, for all that is sacred, let me go in it." She doubts. I insist. I know full well that she is not supposed to do that. The boarding pass for one flight is on no account valid for another. I do not even offer money. I just plead. And she, unaccountably, says I can go on my own responsibility if I really want to. (I shudder now, when recollecting the episode, at the slackness of airline personnel, and at my selfishness to get through against all the rules). I jump ahead, climb the steps and sit in the plane. Then I watch the fun. The crew have done the customary head count, and they have found that there is one head too many. Mine. I sit tight. Over the internal address system comes the captain's voice asking all passengers to keep their tickets ready for examination, as the numbers do not tally. I confidently hand over the counterfoil. My ticket is in perfect order, with the right flight number on it. What is wrong is my boarding pass, but no one asks me that. The tickets are checked, and the plane takes off. I breathe relief. I eat some lunch. The captain's voice comes through again, this time to tell us that mount Kilimanjaro is on the left, and would we care to have a look at it. I do. Then I think of the landing ahead, and my thoughts soon take the shape of prayer. I tell God: "You have my full thanks for this narrow escape. I would have been seriously inconvenienced if I had missed this flight. Bless that charming thoughtless girl who let me through, and forgive the other girl at the counter who distractedly put me in the wrong flight and gave me the wrong boarding pass. I have gone through some anxiety, but I am fine now, and headed for a spotless landing. Only a little point remains, Lord. My luggage. Two bags. A red Samsonite, and a small Air-India overnight bag. I have made it to this flight after some skulduggery, but they haven't. They are on the other

139

flight due to arrive several hours later. And that, again, is going to mean trouble for me and for my hosts. Since I am entering a new country the luggage has to go through customs, that will require my presence at the airport, which means I have to wait there till they come, and the first day's programme will be entirely upset. I don't have many days in Dar-es-Salaam, and if I start badly I could just as well skip the experience. But then, Lord, couldn't you possibly manage it? Don't ask me how you are going to do it, but you are the Lord of the sky and of space, and nothing is impossible for you. If my luggage arrives together with me, I'll be immensely gratified. I leave it to you. And my thanks from now, Lord." These are the days when my own charismatic faith is at its highest as a result of the pentecostal movement that holds me in its full tide. Such a prayer seems perfectly natural to me at the moment, and it gives me peace. We land. I spot my hosts in the visitors' gallery and I wave to them. I go through immigration, and I place myself at the end of the long conveyor belt which has already been set in motion for the luggage of our flight. As I stand at its head my feeling is neatly one of mischievous curiosity. Let me see what happens. It is absurd to expect my bags here. Yet, who knows? Soon I'll be able to tell. I see from far items of luggage beginning to ride on the belt. They come closer. I look carefully. The very first two. Yes. My red Samsonite and the Air-India bag. I pick them up nonchalantly. Anything to declare? No. Welcome to Tanzania. And I walk into the arms of my hosts. That evening is my first talk, and in it I speak of faith, of prayer, of God's power and his readiness to help us in all our needs, big and small. I tell the story of my flight and my luggage. The recent experience has enkindled my faith, and I speak with contagious fervour and deep conviction. The talk livens up, touches many hearts and sets the tone for my whole visit in that new land.

140

It does more than that. At the end of that trip I write a book in Gujarati about it, and a chapter in it is the story of that day as I had lived it and as it had blessed the rest of the trip. Being a writer, my experiences become testimony, and I feel happy to express them in print as I have lived them, however naive they may be. The book has been reprinted, and the story stands.

And now, a couple of years later, I am putting some order in old papers and files and drawers, and I come across an old used air ticket with its luggage tag and boarding card. I recognize the relic as the earthly remains of that memorable flight. But then I notice something I had not noticed on that day. The flight number on the ticket, which was the right one, coincides with the number on the luggage tag, while both differ from the number on the boarding card, which was the one of the wrong flight. And I see it all. As I went to check in in Nairobi, the girl at the counter took my luggage first and booked both the bags for the first flight, as indicated in the ticket. At that moment she was interrupted by another passenger who inquired about the second flight (I distinctly remember the incident), she went back to write my boarding pass, and stamped on it mistakenly the number she had just given in answer to the other man. That is, my luggage was in the right flight from the start, and it was only I who was given the wrong number on my boarding pass. That was the first girl's mistake. When, through the second girl's indulgence, I boarded the first flight, I was only joining my luggage without knowing it. My prayer was certainly heard, two mistakes of two girls cancelling each other, but there was no heavenly jugglery to get my bags to appear with me through clouds and sky. Even their coming out first on the belt was explained by the fact that I was the only passenger in first class, and a first priority red label had been attached to them

141

for preferential delivery. I realize all that when I look at the old tag. No mystery remains. What does remain is the fervour kindled in me by that experience, and the spiritual earnestness it imparted to all my talks and contacts during that trip. The experience was genuine, though the explanation was simple. I wrote it as I felt it at the time. And I write this as I feel it now. One thing I learned: to pay careful attention to the number on the boarding pass at the time of checking in for any flight.

"I tell you this: if you have faith no bigger than a mustard seed, you will say to this mountain, 'Move from here to there!', and it will move."

THOU SHALT REMEMBER

The path of God's people across the desert into the promised land is marked by altars. At important moments in the history of Israel, which is our history, all its great leaders erected altars, and that sacred action was always recorded in the holy books with detailed care, those altars being considered landmarks on the way to liberation. Noah, Abraham, Isaac, Jacob, Moses, Gideon, Samuel, Saul, David, Elijah... built altars on memorable occasions. And the altar is precisely that: a landmark, a milestone, a stone. Something to mark a memorable occasion: a memorial, a monument, a reminder. The altar was not only a place to offer sacrifice, but also and chiefly a solid structure meant to stay, to remain, to be the permanent record of a salvific action, to tell in stone the story of God's wonderful deeds with his chosen people, to be the eternal footprints of the steps of God on earth. In fact at times such stones or pillars were erected without reference to sacrifice, just to mark a place blessed with God's presence and to perpetuate its memory. "Jacob woke from his sleep and said, 'Truly the Lord is in this place, and I did not know it.' Then he was afraid and said, 'How fearsome is this place! This is no other than the house of God, this is the gate of heaven.' Jacob rose early in the morning, took the stone on which he had laid his head, set it up as a sacred pillar and poured oil on the top of it." (Gn 28:16-18). Jacob indeed erected a sacred pillar in every place where he experienced God's help in a special way, and went back to such places to gather strength and revive his faith. God who had helped him in the past would help him also in the future.

That is a great practical way to grow in faith: to remember the past in order to trust for the future. To build altars when we meet God, in order to go back to them when we miss him. Not to repeat our past, which is unique as our future will be, but to find in it the strength to go ahead up to a new victory and a new altar. The roots of our faith are in our past. We are here today because we have believed and we have seen and we have walked. We have all experienced God's salvific action in our lives. There have been days of grace, there have been generous decisions and genuine sacrifices, there have been privileged moments at prayer when all was clear and beautiful and filled with the presence of God, there has been true brotherhood and deep friendship and inward joy. But then, when clouds suddenly cover the sky and darkness invades our lives, we instantly forget all the sunny days and feel desolate and doubt everything and want to give up in despair because nothing works and hope has failed and heaven is closed. In those moments of trial the effective advice is: remember. Bring back to mind the days of light, the moments of bliss, the undeniable certainties, the past victories, and draw the obvious lesson, hidden now from your troubled mind by the present suffering, that what has happened before can happen again, that God who could make his presence felt before in your life can do it any time when he wishes and you are ready,

144

that you do not need anyone to tell you that God helps and prayer works because you have seen it yourself abundantly in your own past. Just remember. And in order to remember, build up altars, put up stones, mark the places in your life where you have met grace and seen the Lord, so that you can go back to them in grateful pilgrimage to regain your strength and rebuild your faith. If Jacob forgets, God will remind him: "I am the God who appeared to you at Bethel where you anointed a sacred pillar and made your vow. Now leave this country at once and return to the land of your birth." (Gn 31:13).

Time and again in Deuteronomy God repeats to his people the commandment that sums up all others: "Thou shalt remember all the way the Lord hath brought thee these forty years" (8:2). The commandment seems at first sight unnecessary. Surely there were in the recent history of the chosen people wonders never to be forgotten, from the Red Sea to the walls of Jericho; still human memory is very very short when it comes to remembering favours and storing graces, and so Israel has to be told: Thou shalt remember. And Moses, conscientious legislator who knew his people and wanted their welfare, insisted clearly before going into detailed legislation: "Take good care: be on the watch not to forget the things that you have seen with your own eyes, and do not let them pass from your minds as long as you live, but teach them to your sons and to your sons' sons. You must never forget." (Dt 4:9-10, 23). Do not forget. If only you remember always the ways of God with you in the past, you will never despair and never lose courage. You have your whole history to back you, your whole life to reassure you. How are you here at all on the way to a new land? Who delivered you from the slavery of a whole world, who fed you, who led you? Have you forgotten so quickly?

145

Is your memory so short? Your tribulations now are not greater than those you suffered before, and I delivered you from those; will you not see, if you only think of that, that I can also deliver you from your present troubles as I did from the past ones? If only you remember your past, you will not fear your future.

St. John of the Cross offers an almost too neat formula to reinforce this thought. "Faith", he says, "is in the understanding, hope in the memory and charity in the will." The scholastic effort to fit the three theological virtues into the three powers of the soul, shows of course, and bespeaks the tastes of the age, but the matching of hope with memory is instructive. Hope, on a first analysis, would seem to be concerned with the future, and it definitely is so, and yet the mystic theologian places hope in the memory. Its roots are in the past, because the ground on which we base our belief that life can bring us joy in the future is our experience that it has done so in the past. That is the mystic's advice: to feel a strong hope, have a good memory.

When many years ago I received my appointment to the missions in India, and was about to leave Spain for the first time in my life, and with it I was leaving too a promising career in the sacred sciences which I was then sacrificing for an unknown future in a remote land, a wise old priest who knew me well and knew the ways of God, uttered a few words I have never forgotten. He told me in that moment of grace, when I was giving up with youthful enthusiasm all that I had, to start the new adventure with no idea of what it was to be, "Remember: God does not do things by halves". I have forgotten almost every other incident of those crowded farewells, but I have always remembered that one. God does not do things by halves. Again, past and future. And the guarantee for the future is the experience of the past. He

146

who has begun, will continue. God is a serious person. He does not begin and leave off. The fact that he has begun is the greatest assurance that he will finish. He has committed himself. His hand is here, and will not be drawn back without accomplishing his work. The rain has left the cloud (Isaiah's image, 55:10), and will not go back without making fertile the earth. God follows up what he begins. Powerful idea that has strengthened me through life. I have prayed it times without number in psalm 138: "The Lord will accomplish his purpose for me. Your true love, O Lord, endures for ever: do not leave unfinished the work of your hands." I have read it in Paul to the Romans: "For the gifts of God and his calling are irreversible" (11:29); and in Peter: "The God of all grace who called you... will confirm and strengthen and perfect you." (1 Pt 5:10); and most forcibly again, in Paul to the Philippians: "Of one thing I am certain: the One who started the good work in you will bring it to completion by the Day of Christ Jesus." (1.6). Beautiful assurance. He who has begun, will bring to completion. God is not like the contractor, derided in the Gospel, who begins to build a tower and leaves it half-way, or like the ploughman who begins to plough and looks back, or like the foolish virgins who brought oil for only half the night. He is thorough, he is reliable, he is God. When he begins, he pledges his word, and his word is certainty. God's beginnings are always auspicious harbingers of a happy end. Bethlehem leads to Jerusalem, and Egypt to Canaan. He will not stop in between. Remember what God has done today to expect what he will do tomorrow. "Remember", the wise old man said at a turning point in my life. I have never forgotten.

The crossing of the Jordan was the decisive step in the pilgrimage of the People of God, the end of the desert journey and the beginning of the final campaign to gain a hold on the land that would be their home. The crossing was attended by a memorable sign. The waters of the river stood still and were cut off so long as the priests carrying the Ark stood in the middle, and the whole people could cross safely on the dry bed. Israel's leader and Moses' successor, Joshua, saw the importance of the event in those crucial days, and the importance of keeping the event ever fresh in Israel's memory to ensure continuity with the past, confidence for the future, fidelity to tradition and loyalty to the group. To obtain that end he used the accepted method of setting up a stone memorial, and he endowed the ceremony with special solemnity. "When the whole nation had finished crossing the Jordan, the Lord said to Joshua, 'Take twelve men from the people, one from each tribe, and order them to lift up twelve stones from this place, out of the middle of the Jordan, where the feet of the priests stood firm. They are to carry them across and set them down in the camp where you spend the night.' Joshua summoned the twelve men whom he had chosen out of the Israelites, one man from each tribe, and said to them, 'Cross over in front of the Ark of the Lord your God as far as the middle of the Jordan, and let each of you take a stone and hoist it on his shoulder, one for each of the tribes of Israel. These stones are to stand as a memorial among you; and in days to come, when your children ask you what these stones mean, you shall tell them how the waters of the Jordan were cut off before the Ark of the Covenant of the Lord when it crossed the Jordan. Thus these stones will always be a reminder to the Israelites.' The Israelites did as Joshua had commanded: they lifted up twelve stones from the middle of the Jordan, as the Lord had instructed Joshua, one for each of the tribes of Israel, carried them across to the camp and set them down there. Those twelve stones are there to this day." (Jos 4:1-9).

148

Joshua was a worthy successor of Moses, and his behaviour on this occasion would be enough to prove it. He leads the people, and at the same time he teaches them. And not only them, but their children and their children's children for ever. He establishes a family catechesis, "when in days to come your children ask you what these stones mean", he builds up a tradition round the twelve stones that were to arouse the curiosity of generations to come, the object lesson, the faithful reminder of a day of glory. We all need those twelve stones in our lives. We all need the sacred memory of the Jordans we have crossed and the battles we have won and the lands we have conquered. We all need the memorial of God's action in our history. So long as the chronicler can write, "and those twelve stones are there to this day", all is well with Israel.

Moses too, before Joshua, had prescribed a similar catechesis on the vital event of the flight from Egypt: the Pasch. "You shall keep this as a rule for you and your children for all time. When you enter the land which the Lord will give you as he promised, you shall observe this rite. Then, when your children ask you, "What is the meaning of this rite?" you shall say, "It is the Lord's Passover, for he passed over the houses of the Israelites in Egypt when he struck the Egyptians but spared our houses." The people bowed down and prostrated themselves." (Ex 12:24-27). The Jewish Pasch was a memorial to keep alive in the minds of the Israelites the day in which they began to be a people. And our Pasch too, our Eucharist, is a memorial: "Do this in memory of me." It, too, has an altar, in every church and in every chapel, and its sight is to remind us, as the altars of the Old Testament, of the great things God has done for us as a people and as individuals, of our history in Christ and our personal experience of him. Every Holy Mass is a reminder,

149

every communion is a summary of past graces and joyful encounters, like meeting an old friend and finding, in the first glance and the first handshake, all the blessed memories that make up a friendship suddenly revived, relived, enjoyed in a mutual emotional celebration of days lived together. Life together is what makes a friendship, and the spontaneous memory of common experiences is the best preparation for future ones. So long as that bond remains, friendship will grow. Faith weakens when memory fails.

When Jesus left the earth, he took care to announce that the Holy Spirit would come "to remind" his disciples (Jn 14:26), to make sure they would not forget. Essential role to build the Church. The Holy Spirit is our faith because he is our memory. Let us never forget.

HE WILL NOT LET ME DOWN

That was a favourite expression with Paul: He will not let me down; he will not fail me; I shall not be put to shame. He had learned it in the Psalms and in Isaiah. "None who look to me will be disappointed" (Is 49:23), "I shall not be put to shame" (50:7), "No man who hopes in you is put to shame" (Ps 25:3), "Let me give my whole heart to your statutes so that I am not put to shame" (119:80), "In you they trusted and were not put to shame" (22:5). And, in contrast, "Let all who worship idols be put to shame" (97:7), "Shame comes to all who break faith with you" (25:3). Paul quotes directly, "Scripture says: Everyone who has faith in him will be saved from shame" (Rm 10:11), "he who has faith in him will not be put to shame" (9:33), and then applies the biblical saying to himself with personal faith and fiery conviction: "I passionately hope I shall never be put to shame" (Ph 1:20). "I know who it is in whom I have trusted, and I am confident of his power to keep safe what he has entrusted to me." (1 T 1:12). Paul undertook heavy labours, met opposition, was in danger of death, but he could face all odds because of his firm belief that the Lord would never let him down.

151

I love to repeat to myself all those texts of Paul and of the Psalms, to pronounce them aloud, to get into their mood, to make them mine; and then to think of the many things, small though they are, that I have undertaken in God's service through my own life. I like to think of the way I have spoken of Jesus to others, the many things I too in my own way have said about Jesus publicly, the way I have proclaimed before others his love, his charm, his power, his grace, my own open commitment to his service, my faith in prayer, my acknowledgement of his Kingdom, the total trust I have professed in his word and his promises and his resurrection and mine through his mercy—and then to pronounce again the words: He will not let me down; I shall not be put to shame; Jesus never disappoints. I do remember that Paul used the expression of his trust in his very last extant letter, writing from jail and facing death. But then the Lord's power extends beyond death, and there too his promise will be gloriously fulfilled and his pledge redeemed. To the last hour of my life he will not let me down.

Jesus is the one who never disappoints. The Jews in Jerusalem paid him that almost reluctant compliment before his last Pasch in the city: "John (the Baptist) gave us no miraculous sign, but all that he said about this man was true." (Jn 10:41). John had said highly encomiastic things of Jesus, had built great expectations around his person, and led people to believe in him though he himself had not seen the signs he had announced; but the people knew and had to recognize at the end that Jesus had fulfilled all that had been said of him. Jesus never disappoints. Jesus never lets down.

All through the Gospel there is a thread of thought that reveals the abundance, the liberality, the exuberance with which God distributes his graces to men, always beyond

152

their expectation. John's prologue: "Out of his full store we have all received grace upon grace"; Jesus to Nathanael: "Because I told you that I saw you under the fig tree you believe? You shall see greater things than that"; the abundance of the best wine at Cana which makes a commentator exclaim after calculating the measures: "No wedding party on earth could drink 180 gallons of wine!"; the catch of fish, so many that "the net begins to tear"; the multiplied loaves, "When I broke the five loaves among five thousand, how many basketfuls of scraps did you pick up? Twelve, they said. And how many when I broke the seven loaves among four thousand? They answered, seven. He said, Do you still not understand?"; how many times must I forgive my brother, seven times? "No, seventy times seven!"; a full day's pay for one hour's work, and "a measure that is full and pressed down and shaken together and running over poured into your lap." Jesus to the Jews: "I have come that men may have life, and may have it in all its fullness"; and to Martha: "Did I not tell you that if you have faith you will see the glory of God?"; and to the Saducees: "You don't know the Scriptures and you don't know the power of God!" It is on that note of overflowing abundance that John ends his Gospel: "There is much else that Jesus did. If it were all to be recorded in detail, I suppose the whole world could not hold the books that would be written." Whatever we know of Jesus and whatever we have experienced of his grace is only a fragment of what he can do and will do with us if we open ourselves to his grace. Jesus never disappoints.

Some of the great parables of Jesus are also, in their first and obvious meaning for the listening crowd, a message of hope and a guarantee of the abundance that surrounds us on all sides when we enter the realm of God's grace and his promises. In the parable of the sower the overwhelming lesson is that whatever the vicissitudes and the labours and frustration of the sowing and tilling and watching through birds and stones and thorns and low-yielding land, the fact is that at the end there is a glorious harvest to rejoice a farmer's heart. The wedding feast cannot be conceived without an abundance of all that is best dispensed without measure. The single coin in the hands of the industrious servant produces ten coins... and he is given ten cities to rule over. The buried treasure is enough to let a man live in luxury for a lifetime. The mustard seed grows irrepressibly into a tree, and the leaven transforms indefectibly the dough into wholesome bread. All through there is a message of hope, of certainty, of abundance, of generosity. Far beyond anything we can claim or imagine. That is the promise of the Kingdom, and the Kingdom is already within us.

A superb text of Paul's. "I pray that your inward eyes may be illumined, so that you may know what is the hope to which he calls you, what the wealth and glory of the share he offers you among his people in their heritage, and how vast the resources of his power open to us who trust in him. They are measured by his strength and the might which he exerted in Christ when he raised him from the dead, when he enthroned him at his right hand in the heavenly realms, far above all government and authority, all power and dominion, and any title of sovereignty that can be named, not only in this age but in the age to come. He put everything in subjection beneath his feet, and appointed him as supreme head to the church, which is his body and as such holds within it the fullness of him who himself receives the entire fullness of God." (Eph 1:18-23). The leisurely reading of Scripture is an outstanding way to grow in faith, and the meditative reading of Ephesians can be a high point in that happy exercise.

154

Paul has another fundamental faith-building concept. That is the idea of God's "fidelity". "God is faithful", "God keeps faith", "God can be trusted", and even when men are faithless, "will their faithlessness cancel the faithfulness of God? Certainly not! God must be true though every man living were a liar." (Rm 3:3). That fidelity of God with himself is the surest foundation of our hope. He is true to himself even when we are not true to ourselves. And then, most interestingly, Paul uses a new term to deepen the same concept, and that is also one of his favourite terms: the justice of God. When we hear "justice" we are inclined to fear, but this justice, on the contrary, is not one that would inspire fear, but hope and confidence and joy. By "the justice of God" Paul does not mean the justice with which God judges us, punishes sin and rewards virtue, but the justice with which he justifies us, the justice with which he makes us just. That is the great manifestation of his mercy and his grace. "But now, quite independently of law, God's justice has been brought to light. The Law and the prophets both bear witness to it: it is God's way of righting wrong, effective through faith in Christ for all who have such faith—all, without distinction. For all alike have sinned, and are deprived of the divine splendour, and all are justified by God's free grace alone, through his act of liberation in the person of Christ Jesus. For God designed him to be the means of expiating sin by his sacrificial death, effective through faith. God meant by this to demonstrate his justice, because in his forbearance he had overlooked the sins of the past—to demonstrate his justice now in in present, showing that he is himself just and also justifies any man who puts his faith in Jesus." (Rm 3:21-26).

The justice of God has been revealed. His salvific plan. His redeeming mercy. It is God's justice that makes us just, removing our doubts, ignoring our unworthiness, cancelling our failures. God's righteousness becomes our surety. That is "God's way of righting wrong, a way that starts from faith and ends in faith". (1:17). God's salvific justice and our personal faith—faith that is acceptance and commitment and action—unite to bring about our redemption.

And now a vital connexion. "These are the words of the Lord: Maintain justice, do the right; for my deliverance is close at hand, and my righteousness (justice) will show itself victorious" (Is 56:1). The verbal play between God's justice that makes us just, and man's justice in dealing fairly with his fellow men is no accident. God's justice in justifying man will show itself victorious when man deals justly with all men, thus showing the effect of God's justice on earth. By faith we make ours God's salvific plan that justifies us, and we implement his justice by working to bring social justice, equality, dignity and freedom to all his children on earth. This will be the last chapter, which, as the scholastic saying has it, was the first to be conceived and the last to be written.

FAITH AND JUSTICE

"Through faith they established justice" (Heb 11:33). That is the concrete summary of the whole history of salvation recapitulated in the names of their main leaders in that crucial chapter eleven of "Hebrews" which has inspired much of my thought in this book. "Faith", there, is the practical trust that God was with them in their lives and their endeavours; and "justice" is the earthly justice to fight for their own and obtain the right to live peacefully in the land God had assigned them. Faith establishes justice by giving strength to fight, confidence into victory and union to live as a people. To obtain justice we must first recover our faith.

Generations of oppression make man lose faith in himself, make him lose his self-respect, his dignity, his identity. The slave comes to regard himself as a slave, and the untouchable as untouchable—and he behaves as such. He is where he belongs (it seems to him), where tradition, caste, the social order or the destiny of humanity have placed him, he himself has come to believe that he is where he ought to be, and so he is the first to oppose change. He does not believe he can ever come out of his plight, and so has ceased to try. Still worse, he rationalizes his own misery, and acquiesces in it, seeking escape in resignation when he has given up the direct line of action. Oppression lowers self-esteem, and low self-esteem facilitates oppression. That vicious circle encloses in its iron grip the whole history of suffering humanity.

To break manfully and once for all this wicked and vicious circle the man under oppression has to conceive again faith in himself, has to see his worth and accept his independence, and the best way for man to acquire faith in himself is to acquire faith in God. If a man sees himself as a child of God and heir to the promises, if he knows himself to be a member of his chosen people in a march of liberation from all chains of body and mind into freedom and grace, if he can personally commit himself to hope and believe in victory and look up to Jesus "in whom faith begins and through whom it reaches its consummation" (12:2), if he brings himself to pronounce and mean and make his own the words that express commitment and lead to action "he will never let me down", then the door is open that leads to hope and to battle and to victory. "This is the victory that overcomes the world: our faith." (1 Jn 5:4). Religious faith is not opium to sedate the masses into conformity, but is dynamite to propel them into action. A person with true faith will never acquiesce in injustice.

Moses, the leader of Israel's liberation, had first formed part of the ruling class in Egypt. He had been "trained in all the wisdom of the Egyptians" (Ac 7:22), "was a very great man in Egypt in the eyes of Pharaoh's courtiers and of the people" (Ex 11:3), and had assumed so fully the ways of living and acting of the Egyptians that people who did not know him, like the daughters of Reuel, took him for an Egyptian (2:19). What awoke him to the reality of injustice

158

and to the need to fight in order to put an end to it was contact with his people. He went to them again, saw by himself their suffering, felt one with them once more, and decided to act. The first condition to work for justice is to witness injustice. Direct contact, personal involvement, presence in the field are the ingredients of awakening. Moses visited his people and threw his lot with them. "One day when Moses was grown up, he went out to his own kinsmen and saw them at their heavy labour. He saw an Egyptian strike one of his fellow-Hebrews. He looked this way and that, and, seeing there was no one about, he struck the Egyptian down and hid his body in the sand. When he went out next day, two Hebrews were fighting together. He asked the man who was in the wrong, 'Why are you striking him?' 'Who set you up as an officer and judge over us?' the man replied. 'Do you mean to murder me as you murdered the Egyptian?' Moses was alarmed. 'The thing must have become known', he said to himself. When Pharaoh heard of it, he tried to put Moses to death, but Moses made good his escape and settled in the land of Midian." (Ex 2:11-15).

Moses identifies with his people. He sheds his Egyptian trappings and becomes one again with the Hebrews. Salvation comes from the inside. No outsider can liberate. Even God to liberate us had to become one of us. Only by being one with those who suffer can we help them free themselves from their sufferings. That may take time and effort and determination, but it is essential and decisive. It is identification that brings redemption.

Moses made mistakes. He was impatient. And violence is the temptation of the impatient man. A gun in the hand is a poor substitute for faith in the heart. The ready shortcut, the single blow. The bomb, the hijack, the war. The killing of the Egyptian. Moses learns early that it does not work.

159

Violence generates violence, and suffering grows. Significantly his own people pointed out to him the weakness of violence: violence, bypassing reason and taking the law into its own hands without a neutral judge, generates mistrust even among one's own people, because if today you use it against an outsider, how do I know you will not use it against me tomorrow? If today you kill an Egyptian, tomorrow you may kill an Israelite. Moses also learned that his own people were quarrelling among themselves. A leader will have to know how to settle disputes. He realizes he needs preparation. Impatience can be beautiful, but formation is of the essence. Moses withdrew into self-exile. It is a characteristic of faith that it knows how to act and it knows how to wait. Moses had already conceived in his heart the irreplaceable desire to free his people. Now he waits to be called. And the day comes.

God calls from the burning bush: "I have indeed seen the misery of my people in Egypt. I have heard their outcry against their slave-masters. I have taken heed of their sufferings, and have come down to rescue them from the power of Egypt, and to bring them up out of that country into a fine, broad land; it is a land flowing with milk and honey, the home of Canaanites, Hittites, Amorites, Perizzites, Hivites, and Jebusites. The outcry of the Israelites has now reached me; yes, I have seen the brutality of the Egyptians towards them. Come now; I will send you to Pharaoh and you shall bring my people Israel out of Egypt." (Ex 3:7-10). The Lord has expressed here what Moses has been feeling in his heart all this time. Yet, when the call comes, Moses hesitates. When the moment for action comes, faith wavers. And Moses draws back: "Who am I to go to Pharaoh? Who am I to bring the Israelites out of Egypt?" There is only one answer to that, and God gives it: "I will be with you." That is faith working for liberation; the premise of faith to give ground and reality to the work of liberation. I will be with you. You, of course, cannot by yourself, but only trust me and believe that I am at your side. I will come and I will act. The proposition is clear, but it has to be fully accepted before God takes charge. The leader's faith has to be strengthened before he can lead. God teaches Moses, and the teaching takes time and even heated exchanges. Moses finds excuses, and God gets angry with him, till finally his firm command overcomes Moses' diffidence. The whole process is instructive to build up leadership in faith. The leader does not impose himself; it is God and circumstances that bring him out. "Moses said, 'O Lord, I have never been a man of ready speech, never in my life, not even now that you have spoken to me; I am slow and hesitant of speech.' The Lord said to him, 'Who is it that gives man speech? Who makes him dumb or deaf? Who makes him clear-sighted or blind? Is it not I, the Lord? Go now; I will help your speech and tell you what to say.' But Moses still protested, 'No, Lord, send whom you will.' At this the Lord grew angry with Moses and said, 'Have you not a brother, Aaron the Levite? He, I know, will do all the speaking. He is already on his way out to meet you, and he will be glad indeed to see you. You shall speak to him and put the words in his mouth; I will help both of you to speak and tell you both what to do. He will do all the speaking to the people for you, he will be the mouthpiece, and you will be the god he speaks for.' " (Ex 4:10-16).

The training was over, and so was the bargaining, and "at length Moses went..." (4:18). Moses now will have to face the might of Pharaoh, the opposition of his courtiers and the scheming of his magicians, and on the other hand the protests, rebellion, jealousy and defeatism of his own people. He has temporary drawbacks and partial failures, the situation of his people becomes even worse for a time after his intervention, and Moses feels frustrated. His own faith is tried, but then he, as Peter would be later, is steadied so that he may steady his brothers. In faith he had been brought up, and in faith he goes on. "By faith, when Moses was born, his parents hid him for three months, because they saw what a fine child he was; they were not afraid of the king's edict. By faith Moses, when he grew up, refused to be called the son of Pharaoh's daughter, preferring to suffer hardship with the people of God rather than enjoy the transient pleasures of sin. He considered the stigma that rests on God's Anointed greater wealth than the treasures of Egypt, for his eyes were fixed upon the coming day of recompense. By faith he left Egypt, and not because he feared the king's anger; for he was resolute, as one who saw the invisible God. By faith he celebrated the Passover and sprinkled the blood, so that the destroying angel might not touch the first-born of Israel. By faith they crossed the Red Sea as though it were dry land, whereas the Egyptians, when they attempted the crossing, were drowned." (Heb 11:23-29). By faith Moses lived and died and led his people into the promise. The greatest work of liberation in sacred history, image and model of all liberations, is summed up in the single word "faith".

In the task of liberating his people, Moses' main concern was to unite them. He knew well that union is essential for liberation. And he knew well that union is difficult. So he applied himself to establish and strengthen the main bond of union, indeed of identity of the people of God, which was faith in Yahweh. The Egyptians had their gods, and every tribe and every nation they would find across the desert and in Canaan would also have its own god. Allegiance defines nationality. Faith fixes frontiers. Moses' unremitting effort will be to keep his people's faith in the one true God against all the temptations that superstitions and images and foreign women and alluring cults will bring to ever fickle minds and fearful hearts. A people that believes becomes one and gathers strength and obtains a land for its own. Faith is the way to justice, the way to liberation, the way to the Promised Land.

Moses has given us the Old Testament model of liberation; and Paul gives us the New Testament model. Moses achieved physical liberation from bodily slavery for the whole people of Israel, and established a free nation in a new land. In the process of building up that nation he gave his people a law to mould their beliefs, rule their behaviour and unify their practices. This new law was originally symbol and instrument of independence, unity and strength. But soon, by the inevitable historical process that transforms initial charism into permanent institution, and inspiration into routine, that very law came to be, as I have explained in earlier chapters, the dark power which, together with sin and death in Pauline thought, represents and effects the deeper slavery of the spirit in bonds of helplessness and misery, never able to be what in its true self it knows it should be and wants to be. Liberation from a law that proclaims obligations without providing the strength needed to fulfill them, and that points out sin only to increase the shame of falling in it, is what Paul proclaims in the name of Christ who "died for our sins and was raised for our justification". (Rm 4:25).

For Paul this liberation from the fundamental oppression of sin was such an overwhelming experience that it overshadowed all other liberations, or rather became the basis and model of them all. The spiritual encounter with

163

Jesus is what marks the soul above all else, and the sense of inner freedom that the believer experiences as a result of it is such that no bondage or oppression can touch him now, since he has been set free for ever in Christ. Paul did know injustice in his day, particularly the most degrading of all injustices man has ever suffered at the hands of man, that is slavery. A slave was not even a person before the law, had no rights, was classified as mere chattel. Aristotle, for all the sublimity of his philosophical thought, divided agricultural implements into three classes: those that had no movement in themselves and no speech, like a plough; those that had movement but no speech, like an ox; and those that had both movement and speech, that is, slaves. Intolerable situation to which Christianity had to react. Christianity, based on the principle that we are all children of God, declared from its very beginning the radical equality of all men and women, to the extent that in Christ "there is no such thing as Jew and Greek, slave and freeman, male and female" (Gal 3: 28). There was, however, no initial move to abolish or denounce slavery. The important thing for Paul was to claim and feel that essential freedom in Christ which makes even the slave and prisoner free. I quote from M. Carrez in "Vocabulary of the Bible": "The first communities were faced with some very delicate problems. Some slaves had become Christians, while their owners had remained pagans: what should be their proper attitude? Some Christians owned pagan slaves: what were they to do? For the apostle Paul, 'Christ died for all, that those who live might live no longer for themselves but for him who for their sake died and was raised' (2 Cor 5:15). The end of life is communion with Christ (Rm 10:10-13). Emancipation from slavery remains secondary. 'For he who was called in the Lord as a slave is a freedman of the Lord. Likewise he who was free when called is a slave of Christ... In whatever state

164

each was called, there let him remain with God' (1 Cor 7:22,24). In Christ there is no longer master or slave (Gal 3:28). Let each master remember his heavenly Master. Let the slave have always before his eyes the example of Christ, the true servant (Ph 2:5-11). It is not indifference to social questions, since both the slaves and their owners are exhorted to live in Christ (cf. Col 3:22-4:1; Eph 6:5-9), but rather a translation into the terms of social existence of the love of the Father (the only true Master) for the Son (the only true servant) and *vice versa*. The apostle Paul does not lay down general instructions, but gives encouragement. He was not, in the modern sense of the word, a revolutionary, still less a traditionalist. He sought to emphasize that what had to be worked out in daily life was the extraordinary fact that in Christ all men, masters or slaves, were one. But this is a far larger reality than any simple claims on the human level: these are not overlooked, but they are relegated to their proper station: they belong to a transitory order (1 Cor 7:31)."

Two considerations help us to understand why Paul did not directly oppose the institution of slavery as we with our present outlook would have liked him to do. One, that he was a child of his time, moving among the social institutions of his day without a direct mission to overturn them; and, two, that he personally believed that the end of the world was near, and so there was no point in advocating radical changes. "The time we live in will not last long. While it lasts, married men should be as if they had no wives...; buyers must not count on keeping what they buy, nor those who use the world's wealth on using it to the full. For the whole frame of this world is passing away." (1 Cor 7:29-31). But there is a third consideration which I have pointed out just now, and which to my mind is the key to Paul's attitude: the reality of the outpouring of the Spirit which he himself had experienced and had led others to experience was so blissfully overwhelming that everything else paled into insignificance before that, and a person who had received the Spirit could cheerfully afford to bypass material considerations of status and rank. This is a dangerous statement, and an important one. I say it is dangerous because it could be interpreted to mean that spiritual considerations could lead us to ignore human needs, and ministration to the soul render void the claims of the body and of the mind in physical want and social oppression. In other words, that we can forget the "body" so long as we properly look after the "soul". That meaning would be entirely wrong, and if the shadow of it would fall on the teaching and the experience of the apostle it would invalidate from the start its message for us today. And I say that the statement is important because we need it in order to restore the balance between pastoral work and social work, to use a generally accepted and quickly understood terminology, or rather to blend a unity out of the two. The urgency of man's needs today in daily bread and social equality and human dignity is so genuine and so glaring that it tends to take easy preference over his no less genuine need of faith to hold on to joy, and prayer to hold on to faith; and he and his liberators may choose the immediate road to quick delivery from external evils rather than the winding road of interval deliverance from his own fears and doubts and compulsions. It is easier to give a man bread than to teach him to pray. And it is not possible to teach him to pray on an empty stomach. We need both the prayer and the bread. Only let us not forget the prayer.

Paul's principle "stay the way you are", which played an important part in his teaching to all the churches, was no defeatism or indifference before social inequalities, but, on the contrary, an act of faith in the power of the Spirit who can act in any human situation, even the most degrading one, and can make a man be and feel supremely free even when apparently he is a slave. That is the basic reality on which every concrete movement of total liberation will stand and be built when the conscience of men awakens as we are happily experiencing in our days. Paul's thought is clearly that the slave need not wait till his chains are removed in order to be and feel fully and totally man, but that, since the moment he has met God in Christ, he is already, in faith and in experience, a perfect man, a free person, and a son of God; and, as a consequence of that intimate conscience of freedom that grows in him and spreads through society, his chains will fall one day when humanity ripens and Christian values begin to rule the behaviour of men. For Paul it would be lack of faith to say that a slave cannot feel fully a man unless he ceases being a slave. That would be underestimating the power of redemption, denying that a slave can be a "freedman in Christ", as Christ himself was God on the cross, and conditioning the freedom of the spirit to the welfare of the body. And for us, on whom a new fullness of time has dawn in social conscience and liberating action, it would be lack of faith to leave the slave in his chains and not to do all we possibly can to remove them. The danger is that the activity necessary to break the chains may make us forget the deeper need of the inner liberation. Both liberations are needed, and the inner one is the basis and soul of the outer one. That is Paul's concern.

Paul had felt the power of the Spirit in himself ("whether in the body or out of the body, I don't know, God knows"), in his work and in his churches. "I have been Christ's instrument to bring the Gentiles into his allegiance, by word and deed, by the force of miraculous signs and by the power of the Holy Spirit." (Rm 15:18-19). "By a display of the power of the Spirit." (1 Cor 2:5). "The marks of a true apostle were there, in the work I did among you, which called for such constant fortitude, and was attended by signs, marvels and miracles." (2 Cor 12:12-13). "God gives the Spirit and works miracles among you." (Gal 3:5). "We brought you the Gospel in the power of the Spirit." (1 Th 1:5). The epistle to the Hebrews speaks of "the spiritual energies of the age to come" which had already manifested themselves publicly in that first apostolate. (Heb 6:5). And the book of Acts, almost step-by-step biography of pauline apostolate, marks the stages of his preaching with the interventions of the divine power that confirmed it. Already in Cyprus the hand of the Lord blinded Elymas who opposed Paul (13:10); in Iconium "the Lord confirmed the message of his grace by causing signs and miracles to be worked at their hands" (14:3); at Lystra Paul cured a crippled man, lame from birth, who had never walked in his life (14:8); in Philippi an earthquake freed him from jail (16:26); in Ephesus "God, through Paul, worked singular miracles: when handkerchiefs and scarves which had been in contact with his skin were carried to the sick, they were rid of their diseases and the evil spirits came out of them" (19:11); at Troas he returns young Eutychus to life after he had fallen from a third-storey window and picked up for dead (20:12). Well could Paul sum up his preaching not as an efficient campaign ("I came before you weak, nervous, and shaking with fear") but as a "display of the power of the Spirit". (1 Cor 2:3-5). The experience of the Spirit in himself and in others was the essential element in Paul's life and work, and all his attitudes and reactions to problems and events in his time have to be placed against that background if they are to be properly understood.

The very letter in which Paul says, "let each one remain in the condition in which he was when he was called", which is his first to Corinth, is the letter where he describes the joy of the charisms and the bursting energy of a new Church in prophecy and tongues, in miracles and healings, and in the glorious vitality of their weekly meetings. Every meeting of the Church of Corinth was an event, and every Eucharist a feast. The Spirit of God moved freely among those first Christians, in their hearts and in their tongues, in their meetings and in their worship, in their prayers and in all their lives, and it was easy under the guidance and with the strength of the Spirit to give meaning to any situation and to find joy even in adverse circumstances. An inner liberation had been experienced which led the Corinthian Christian to view his life in a new light, and to be free to react by effecting a change or by choosing continuity without any compulsion for either.

Each Corinthian meeting must have been a holy riot of spiritual joy that burst into voices and gestures, healings and prophecies, inspired prayers and mutual exhortations to such an extent that it became difficult to put order in all that and satisfy everybody. Paul brings in that context the comparison with the human body where quite different members and organs harmonically cooperate to the welfare of all by carrying out each one his own function; then he insists on love, with almost poetical mysticism in his outpouring, as the supreme principle that has to give order and unity to the whole life and activity of the person and of the group; and finally gives even practical rules (let them speak by turn, let no more than two or three prophesy, let the women not speak...) and ends by requesting them to do everything "properly and in order". (1 Cor 14:40). The interest that Paul manifests and the space he takes up with

169

that matter are some indication of the great importance such a phenomenon had, and they give us the atmosphere and background, unfortunately lost to us, against which all the other teachings of Paul in the same letter have to be placed if we want to profit by them. The Corinthian Christians had undergone a very deep transformation both in their private and in their social life, and they had achieved such an internal freedom that they could see life and its situations in another light, and felt supremely free to choose a new way or to remain in an old one without any pressure from outside whether for novelty or for tradition. Theirs was the ultimate liberty of the children of God. The Christian, whatever he is and wherever he is, is already a citizen of heaven. (Eph 2:19).

In Corinth itself Paul had to handle a sensitive problem, which has a bearing on this same situation, and he addresses himself to it in the same letter. For the "fraternal meal" that accompanied the celebration of the Eucharist, well-to-do Christians were bringing with themselves and consuming before the others generous supplies of food and drink, while poor Christians went hungry by their side. And Paul's solution is: "Eat at home." Here again we, with out present-day social awareness, would have preferred him to say: "Take out what you all bring, and share it equally among yourselves." And again that would be imposing on Paul our circumstances and our outlook, and missing what, even with our present awareness, is still an important lesson for us too. Paul's main concern at that moment was the Eucharist, which was truly a celebration, a rejoicing, a peak experience each time in the routine of life, a date to look forward to, a source of strength for each Christian and the centre and heart of the local Church. That had to be safeguarded by all means, and Paul's injunction achieves just that. He did have a concern for the poor too, and indeed he carried out a lifelong campaign to collect funds for the poor Christians in Jerusalem; but his great care was for the gift of the Spirit and the building of the Church, and he knew that a live Eucharist was essential for that. Therefore he takes care of the Eucharist first.

Our own Eucharists are not often Corinthian Eucharists, and as a compensation we may find ourselves taking more care of the "fraternal meal", organizing the sharing of what each one can contribute, and making sure that nobody goes back hungry... in his stomach, while many go back hungry in their souls. We do not find it easy to prepare the people for the gift of the Spirit, and may take instead to organizing them for protest or for action. That action is fine; but not as a substitute for the Spirit. We priests have lost spiritual power among the people of God, and the growing temptation in our souls is to make up for that loss by going in for other kinds of power: material power, group power, money power, and, to say the ultimate word, political power. I repeat with clarity and boldness: what that power and action are in themselves and in the effects they bring about can all be and often is very positive, urgent and necessary, and it involves hard work and at times even heroic sacrifices; but the exercise and the results of such power and action will never compensate mankind and the world for the loss of spiritual power in the people who have been chosen to be its consecrated channels. There is no replacement for a Corinthian Eucharist.

In the struggle for "faith and justice" we have only too often isolated "justice" and forgotten "faith". I chose carefully the title of this book to reflect my own thinking from the start and to state my thesis clearly: "Faith *for* Justice." The ultimate aim is justice, but the search for justice has to be

171

imbued from the very beginning with explicit faith that will infuse it with meaning, lend it power and give it life. The experience of faith in all its varied richness and stark depth is the essential component of the thrust for social justice and human dignity, both in those who promote the thrust and in those who integrate it. The basic liberation of the spirit, ground and essence of all other liberations, or, rather, soul of the only total liberation that frees the whole of man in all that he is and can be, and of which all other liberations are glimpses and signs, is the first and irreplaceable requirement for all those involved in the righteous fight for justice, the leaders and the led. The hand that distributes the bread to the hungry who cannot wait, has to be led by the heart that believes that there is love in the world and justice in heaven, and that through that gesture, immediate and imperative, proclaims the concrete hope for problems which all statesmen of the world together have been unable to solve. And the hungry man, once his overpowering need has been satisfied, can see in the hand that fed him with bread and with love, that in the midst of all the direst needs and despairing situations of a world gone mad, there is the possibility of coming out of misery and looking up in hope and working for equality and being fully man. The leader needs faith to shoulder a seemingly impossible task, and the people need all the more faith to believe after so many false promises, and to let hope unite them in the common upheaval that is already shaking the world. We have to build up a just world, urgent privilege that the course of history has thrown into our feeble hands, and to that task we want to consecrate the whole of our lives. That is why it is essential to remind ourselves that without faith, that building will go up without its foundations. Without faith we cannot achieve justice. Paul says epigrammatically that the only thing that matters is "faith active in love" (Gal 5:6). After walking side by side with him in many pages of this book, I feel emboldened to adapt his wording: "faith active in justice". That sums up the whole.

I want to make this point even clearer before I end. I have derived great personal profit from reading excellent books on 'Liberation Theology' and living close to people who are generously and intelligently engaged in the best work for total liberation amongst the most destitute people on earth. I have discovered a new depth and unity in Scripture, from Exodus through Psalms and Prophets to Apocalypse, and I have felt the sudden challenge of interpreting God's action with his People, not only as an external image to show visibly in material liberation a model and hope of the spiritual liberation in the heart of man (Israel is freed from the power of Pharaoh as the soul is freed from the power of sin), but as a reality to be repeated through history and to be carried out in our days by freeing the victims of injustice from the bonds that enslave them in body and soul.

I have felt the tension, common to all who work in the field today in one way or another, between the two realities that liberation terminology has expressed as the "transformation of structures" and the "conversion of hearts". The latter expression corresponds to "faith" in the vocabulary of this book, while the former is "justice" in its concrete social application. We all stress now one now the other as we react to situations which call for thought and action in real urgent needs, and we all seek the living synthesis that will bring balance and effectiveness to our own approach.

That is why I rejoiced when I read in the *"Instruction on Christian Freedom and Liberation"* of the Congregation for the Doctrine of Faith, dated 22 March 1986, the words: "It is therefore necessary to work simultaneously for the conversion of hearts and for the improvement of structures" (no. 75).

173

And in a study on the same Instruction I came across the following words of H. Büchele: "The change of structures without man's change of himself is a materialistic or collective illusion. The change of self and person without the change of structures is an idealistic or liberalistic illusion." We need both faith and justice to respond fully to the vital needs of society today. In this book I have focussed my attention on faith to show how the call to justice fits into the fundamental call to faith, and acquires in it all the depth of meaning and urgency of action which we are privileged to feel in our hearts today.

For me this essential linkage between justice and faith is just obvious and evident, essential rule and fundamental analysis for any work of personal growth or social liberation. If any liberation activity is "from faith to faith" (Rm 1:17), it will strike root and spread out and bear fruit. And I apply confidently this criterion to others because I have been applying it to myself and to my work for years. I have asked myself time and again with growing intensity and searching sincerity the question: What do I really want when I work with people and for people, when I go to visit them, to talk with them or to give talks to them, when I give them my ideas and listen to them and pray with them, what do I want them to retain in their memory about me when they forget all the mathematics I have taught them in the class-room, what do I want to give to people who know me and meet me and listen to me and read me? And the answer I have given myself consistently through the years is: I want to give them faith. Faith in life, faith in themselves, in other men, in society, in creation, in God. I want that little woman who looks tired and haggard with the day's work and life's burden when I enter her house, to look up and smile and feel light and welcome life and know that her toiling has a meaning

174

and her worth is appreciated and she has the right to ask for her own and satisfy her needs and enjoy things in the measure that is fit for her. I want that young man who frets at his own inadequacy and at mankind's troubles and comes to talk about them with aggressive impatience, to realize that he can do much if only he reconciles himself to himself and learns to trust himself and to trust God who loves him and will give him the strength he needs to go ahead and find a way and do good to others and help mankind and brighten his own life. I want the mature man who has seen everything and is disappointed with everything and drags his existence along in a drab world, to rediscover life and see the sun and recover faith in the human race and in the goodness of things and in the love of God. I want all men and women in today's world to be moved, awaken, sensitized to the presence of opresion in man's heart and in society's structures, and so to move concertedly and effectively to remove the causes of suffering and to build a happier world based on a just society. And I want myself to keep my eyes open and see the hand of God in human events and the breath of his Spirit in the yearnings of man, to feel his presence in my breast and his whisperings in my heart, to recognize his voice in every word of Scripture and his touch in every Eucharist, to see his image in every human face and his Passion in every suffering, and to hope and proclaim and grasp and live already his blessed Resurreccion in the faith and assurance that the kingdom has come because the King is here, and with him, in sign and seed and pledge, the final justice that is meant to reach all men and redeem the earth, and for which we have to keep on working heart and soul while we are in this world which God has made for men and women to love each other and him in it.

I have always looked on faith as the summary of my life. That is why I had a great desire to write this book.

175